AWAY WITH WORDS

Young Writers' 16th Annual Poetry Competition

It is feeling and force of imagination that make us eloquent.

How can I not dream while writing? The blank page gives a right to dream.

Verses From The West Midlands
Edited by Annabel Cook

First published in Great Britain in 2007 by:
Young Writers
Remus House
Coltsfoot Drive
Peterborough
PE2 9JX
Telephone: 01733 890066
Website: www.youngwriters.co.uk

All Rights Reserved

© *Copyright Contributors 2007*

SB ISBN 978-1 84602 805 2

Foreword

This year, the Young Writers' *Away With Words* competition proudly presents a showcase of the best poetic talent selected from thousands of up-and-coming writers nationwide.

Young Writers was established in 1991 to promote the reading and writing of poetry within schools and to the young of today. Our books nurture and inspire confidence in the ability of young writers and provide a snapshot of poems written in schools and at home by budding poets of the future.

The thought, effort, imagination and hard work put into each poem impressed us all and the task of selecting poems was a difficult but nevertheless enjoyable experience.

We hope you are as pleased as we are with the final selection and that you and your family continue to be entertained with *Away With Words Verses From The West Midlands* for many years to come.

Contents

Hillcrest School, Birmingham

Kate Yeomans (11)	1
Lucy Need (11)	2
Jaya Kumar (11)	3
Akira Jeffers (11)	4
Emma Goora (11)	5
Bethany Baker (11)	6
Morgan James (11)	7
Rebecca Small (11)	8
Hannah Buckley-Mellling (12)	9
Sadia Abid (11)	10
Deborah Olaiya (11)	11
Priya Gil (11)	12
Jamie Grant (12)	13
Ala Saif (11)	14
Hiba Al-Byati (12)	15
Jung Min Woo (11)	16
Laylaa Douglas (12)	17
April Burrows (11)	18
Neree McKenzie (13)	19

Kingsbury School & Sports College, Erdington

Tim Guest (11)	20
Zhan'e Burke (11)	21
Ashley Steer (11)	22
Scott Evans (11)	23
Amy Johnson (11)	24
Tain Leavy (12)	25
Demileigh Collins (12)	26
Danielle Harvey (12)	27
Nur Izzati Mohamad Hariri (13)	28
Kelly Shale (12)	29
Leanne Lowe (12)	30
Bethany Joesbury (12)	31
Danielle Pryor (11)	32
Sakub Yasin (11)	33
Kimberley Buck (12)	34
Charlotte Beirne (11)	35
Leona Taylor (11)	36

Name	Page
Brett Bick (11)	37
Aaron Lovell (11)	38
Chloe-Anne Holmes (12)	39
Christopher Hickman (12)	40
Paige Hunter (12)	41
Joanna Parkes (12)	42
Sophie Brown (14)	43
Zoe Peters (14)	44
Sigourney Gerald (15)	45
Rochelle Johnson (15)	46
Lauren Wilding (14)	47
Sarah Smart (14)	48
Adam Pietrzak (14)	49
Hasan Mahmood (14)	50
Sophie Cox (14)	51
Pooja Gill (12)	52
Reece Weston (11)	53
Ruth Dixon (12)	54
Megan Beckley (11)	55
Sadé Robinson (12)	56
Matthew Cross (13)	57
Davaine Whyte (15)	58
Jennifer Horspool (11)	59
Bethany Wignall (11)	60
Talia Ali (11)	61
Charlie-Shauna Wager (12)	62
Jordan Lovell (11)	63
Gemma Johnson (15)	64
Helena Borthwick (14)	65
Claire Griffiths (14)	66
Kalesha Palmer (14)	67
Jadine Ijoyah (11)	68

Ninestiles Technology College, Acocks Green

Name	Page
Lakvinder Kaur (12)	69
Whitney Donaldson (11)	70
Amy Boland (11)	71
Gurpreet Rathore (12)	72
Elizabeth Gould (12)	73
Madeleine Levy (16)	74
Laura Brinkworth (13)	75

Aishah Mahmood (13)   76
Stacie Hughes (13)   77
Rachel Hanrahan (13)   78

Oldbury College of Sport, Oldbury

Amie Spencer (14)   79
Alex Wood (12)   80
Jason Booth (11)   81
Raekwon Douglas (12)   82
Ellouise Wheelwright (11)   83
Leah Ainge (12)   84
Alice Rowley (12)   85
Rebekah Massy (12)   86
Lyle Farnell (12)   87
Leena Sharma (12)   88
Lamis Amireh (11)   89
Sofia Butt (14)   90
Laura Wilcox (13)   91
Olivia Wright (14)   92
Sabrina Kumari (12)   93
Paul Hughes (13)   94
Jordan Gibbs (12)   95
Megan Hill (12)   96
Amanda Sears (12)   97
Beth Chantler (13)   98
Gurpreet Ghuman (12)   99
Rebecca Pearsall (11)   100
Ashleigh Barratt (11)   101
Sadie Redding (13)   102
Jasmyn Williams (11)   103
Amy Spence (13)   104
Gemma White (14)   105
Sophie Powell (13)   106
Belise Nirin Giyimana (13)   107
Gemma Giles (14)   108
Bethany Littleton (12)   109
Aaron Randhawa (12)   110
Leah Elsworth (12)   111
Kierron Barker (12)   112
Abbie-Leigh Allard (13)   113

Kieron Cherrington (12) — 114
Kirandeep Kaur (13) — 115

Perryfields High School, Oldbury
Amrit Kaur (13) — 116
Ashleigh Simpson (13) — 117
Chantelle Warren (13) — 118
Amrita Phull (13) — 119
Emma Leppington (16) — 120

Queen Mary's High School, Walsall
Sunayna Shinh (12) — 121
Lauren Garbett (11) — 122
Seliesha Chahal (12) — 123
Zoë Nicholson (17) — 124
Lauren Key (12) — 125
Georgina Edkins (12) — 126
Kate Bradley (13) — 127
Stacy Knight (17) — 128
Daisy Hale (12) — 129
Kanem Hutchinson (13) — 130
Lauren Smith (13) — 131
Erin Charles (14) — 132
Amy Kular (12) — 133
Chloë Guy (13) — 134
Bonnie Tsim (11) — 135
Caitlin Clarke (13) — 136
Laura Pincher (12) — 137
Alysia Dyke (11) — 138
Vincy Lee (12) — 139
Anika Loi (12) — 140
Taranpreet Kaur Sohal (11) — 141
Nikita Joshi (11) — 142

Smestow School, Castlecroft
Anil Bansal (11) — 143
Katy Skobel (11) — 144
Ophiah Deans (11) — 145
Tarnia Osborne (11) — 146
Ryan Silwood (11) — 147
Gurgeena Bhadal (11) — 148

Michael Williams (15) 149
Hollie Brown (11) 150
Michael Jukes 151
Abbie Jane Robinson (11) 152
Vishaal Leekha (11) 153
Joe Ellam (11) 154

Solihull Sixth Form College, Solihull
Sophie Deery (16) 155

The Orchard Centre PRU, Wolverhampton
Andrew Osborne (12) 156
Daniel Howells (13) 157
Joshua Williams (13) 158
Ryan Weston (13) 159
Elizabeth Homer (13) 160
Samantha Hughes (13) 161
Christopher Parker (12) 162
Mikey Howells (11) 163
Elizabeth Price (15) 164
Jordan Dearn (13) 165

Warley High School College of Sport, Oldbury, Oldbury
Stacey Kendrick (13) 166
Priya Thamilarasan (13) 167
Demi Woodward (13) 168
Rachel Bayliss (13) 169
Ayshea Ravenscroft (13) 170
Ashlee Carver (13) 171
Gemma Brookes (13) 172
Ivinder Virdee (13) 173
Danielle Watton (13) 174
Lydiarose Smith (13) 175
Charlotte Woolls (13) 176
AZB (13) 177
Emma Bate (13) 178
Emma Harley (13) 179
Charlie Morrall (13) 180
Mollie Bastable (13) 181

Whiteheath Education Centre, Rowley Regis
    Lucy Botfield (14)   182
    Elizabeth Worton (13)   183
    Kyle Roberts (13)   184
    Lee Dyson (13)   185
    Amy Dyson (13)   186

The Poems

My Brother

He looked after me
When I was small,
Played with dolls,
Books and more.

He gave me love
When I was ill,
Gave me medicine,
Juice and pill.

When he left home
I cried and cried,
My best friend was gone,
Not by my side.

He's older now
And soon to be a dad,
But he's the best brother,
Anyone could have!

Kate Yeomans (11)
Hillcrest School, Birmingham

Pets

P ets are for life not just for Christmas.
E veryone waits for the love of a home.
T ake one of us pets in and you'll never go kissless.
S o long as you treat us as one of your own, for now
and forever in your home.
From cute cuddle cats to fun-loving dogs to big hairy spiders
to slimy green frogs.

Lucy Need (11)
Hillcrest School, Birmingham

The Loveliest Thing In The World!

The loveliest thing
in the world
has got to be the
prettiest.

The loveliest thing
in the world
has got to be
the most calming.

The loveliest thing
in the world
has got to be
the nicest.

The loveliest thing
in the world
has got to be
your *smile*.

Nothing in the
world can be
better than a
smiling face.

Jaya Kumar (11)
Hillcrest School, Birmingham

The Fright Of Hallowe'en

Hallowe'en night
All was quiet
Argh!
Was that a pirate?

Silence hustles
In the night
Everybody gets a fright.

What is that
On the church spire?
Could it be a vampire?

Everybody gets a fright

Especially on Hallowe'en night. . .

Akira Jeffers (11)
Hillcrest School, Birmingham

Witches Brew

Bubble, bubble
Boil and double
Potion sizzle
And please don't drizzle

A dying chicken's bloody guzzard
A toenail of an ugly wizard
And a foot of a deep fried lizard.

A reddish rose pulled from the roots
A piece of fabric from a mail man's boots
And don't forget a couple of newts.

Fur from a witch's cat
Foot of a blood-sucking bat
And a tail of an oversized rat.

And at last a petal wrapped in foil
And a couple of handfuls of soil.

Emma Goora (11)
Hillcrest School, Birmingham

If Only

I wish I hadn't done that
I wish I hadn't tried
If only I had waited
And now my hands are tied!

It started just this morning
The one today you know!
Time passed me so quickly
Yet I was moving slow.

We went to church this morning
And everything went fine
Until 'The man' came in the room
In his hand a great vine.

He swung it round so violently
Till everyone stood still
The terror of the room was to his every single will!

I tiptoed o so quietly
I didn't want him to see
That I wanted to leave the room
To get help and set us free!

It wasn't at all to be that way
I wasn't to get out at all!
He saw me, o yes he saw me
And all I could do was fall.

If only I hadn't done that!
(whack)
He made no exception for me!

Bethany Baker (11)
Hillcrest School, Birmingham

Life

Life is hard
Life is rough,
The floors are dirty
The floors are tough.

Jagged and sharp
On your feet,
Giving you blisters
They didn't look sweet.

Walking slowly
But you looked so lonely.

Morgan James (11)
Hillcrest School, Birmingham

My Chocolate Candy Heaven

My chocolate candy heaven,
I dream every night.
I love my chocolate people,
My dolly mixture animals but
Especially the eatable houses.

My chocolate candy heaven,
I just can't wait to dream.
I hear the milk chocolate droplets,
I love its snow, it's a white chocolate snow
And I enjoy the Coca-Cola swimming pools!

My chocolate candy heaven,
I really wish it was real!
I wish Willy Wonka was alive,
He would make brilliant chocolate,
No one would say chocolate's nasty!

Rebecca Small (11)
Hillcrest School, Birmingham

Little Miss Hilton

Little Miss Hilton loves her poochie
And also adores wearing Gucci,

She roams around the streets at night
Whilst waiting to catch her Hollywood flight,

She flights away in her own private jet
And whatever she wants she'll get, get, get,

Money this, money that,
Clothes this, clothes that,

Her favourite items are shoes of course
But when she was little she never wanted a horse,

All she wanted was designer stuff
And if she didn't get it she went off in a huff,

Bracelets, necklaces and diamond rings
These are all some of her favourite things.

Hannah Buckley-Mellling (12)
Hillcrest School, Birmingham

Children! Children! Children!

Throwing paper planes
across the classroom
being a real pain
Children! Children! Children!

I wish I stayed at home
relaxing in my bed
I just want to be alone!
Children! Children! Children!

Running around
teasing each other
in the playground
Children! Children! Children!

They chew gum
making lots of terrible noise
and they also hum
Children! Children! Children!

I've had enough
I can't take it anymore
this class is tough
I'm quitting, bye-bye!

Sadia Abid (11)
Hillcrest School, Birmingham

GCSEs

Reading and reading for GCSEs
Seems all too much to read
Reading and reading for GCSEs
The day has come for the test,
So nervous, so nervous
What shall I do GCSES?
Just do your best, just do your best.
Working out, working out the answers
All I have to do is wait.
Finished waiting, the letter has come
Opening it as slow as I can
Then all I see to see is AAA
Worth it reading, worth it reading
Thank you, thank you GCSEs.

Deborah Olaiya (11)
Hillcrest School, Birmingham

Refugee!

R epeating wanting to go home.
E ndlessly crying for help.
F rightened.
U pset.
G oing mad.
E ating nothing at all.
E nd of my life.

Priya Gil (11)
Hillcrest School, Birmingham

My Grandad

My grandad was kind and loving
he was grateful and good-hearted
he was stubborn and never took any notice of anybody
and he was always good-natured.

We always used to fight and argue over the Galaxy chocolate
he was like a little child again.

We used to go swimming together
watch TV together
and make wine together.

I miss my grandad
and I wish he was still alive
to see me today.

Jamie Grant (12)
Hillcrest School, Birmingham

Flowers

They're colourful and bright
They attract bees' sight
Don't worry they don't sting
They're only little things

Watch out for pollen
It will really make you sneeze
Your nose will go swollen
Achoo, Achoo, Achoo

Pollen gave me sneezes
And then I got wheezes
Then I had to stay home
All . . . on . . . my . . . own!

Ala Saif (11)
Hillcrest School, Birmingham

Detention

Maths, Maths, Maths,
'So I said' I'd rather sit on mats
So I told the teacher, what I couldn't mention
So then I get detention!

English, English, English,
'So I said' I'd rather eat some fish *(eeewww)*
So I told the teacher that 'English is my doom,'
So she sent me to the naughty room!

Science, Science, Science,
'So I said' I'd rather work with clients
So I told the teacher, 'I'd rather get polluted,'
So she told me that I was excluded!

Hiba Al-Byati (12)
Hillcrest School, Birmingham

What A Wonderful Happening!

The sun rises,
The moon goes down,
Flowers bloom,
The winds blow,
What a wonderful happening!

And, when wind is blowing
Pollen flies and falls down to the ground
Shoots grow on trees
What a wonderful happening!

Whatever, whenever
People must not disturb this
Earth's happening.

Jung Min Woo (11)
Hillcrest School, Birmingham

Mother's Day Poem

Coffee drinker,
Excellent thinker,
Chocolate eater,
Material pleater,
Good cooker,
Conscious looker,
Shoe buyer,
Chip fryer,
Expert shopper,
Money dropper,
Bird lover,
Cat hugger,
House cleaner,
Sewing machiner.

I love you mom.

Laylaa Douglas (12)
Hillcrest School, Birmingham

Butterfly

They gracefully fly,
Their delicate wings.
What can it be but a butterfly?
So many of them.
So many colours you can see
From the rainbow in the sky.
What can it be?
A butterfly.

April Burrows (11)
Hillcrest School, Birmingham

Emotions

Passion is intensity
Don't feel tense
Power is pain
Your life is not in vain
Fear is danger
Don't worry you're not a stranger
Stumble and fall
You've got a friend you can call.

Neree McKenzie (13)
Hillcrest School, Birmingham

Me!

As long as I live
I shall always be
Myself - and no other
Just me

Like a monkey
Growing stronger
Step by step
To a gorilla

Like a team
Growing stronger
Trying to win the league
Playing better each game.

Or a soldier
Battling for his country
Doing anything to survive.

And that's me
Till the day I die
When my soul is gone
I may rest in peace.

Tim Guest (11)
Kingsbury School & Sports College, Erdington

Me!

From when we were born
till death do us part
me and my spirit
will never depart.

I am a tree, we are a tree
with a big strong bark
or maybe an oak tree
or just me.

Or maybe an animal
a lion that can roar loud
or a cheetah that can run fast
or just me.

So now can you see,
it's all just me
it's all me
me, my soul and my body.

Zhan'e Burke (11)
Kingsbury School & Sports College, Erdington

Me

As long as I live
I shall always be myself
and no one else

Like an oak big and strong
and the trunk thick and long
like a daffodil tall and bright
when dark it searches for light

I'm like the sea sometimes calm
and sometimes rough
I am like a bear
but without the hair

In the future I will have kids
hopefully win my bids
but life isn't all about money
it's to be happy!

Ashley Steer (11)
Kingsbury School & Sports College, Erdington

As Long As I Live

As long as I live
I shall always be
myself no other
just me.

Like a tree
tall, hard
strong and
helpful.

Like a tiger
big sharp teeth
big, strong, lazy
and sometimes very hyper.

Always the same
even when I
grown up and
get a job
even when I
die I will
never change.

Scott Evans (11)
Kingsbury School & Sports College, Erdington

Me!

As long as I live
I will always be me
nobody else just me
always me.

Like a flower
growing
in its own unique way
with its own colours.

Like a bird
soaring through the sky
free as a butterfly
free flying through the air.

Always going to be me
never going to change
unique
only one
that's me.

Amy Johnson (11)
Kingsbury School & Sports College, Erdington

Zante!

Zante is an amazing place
It gives you a happy face
It has amazing branded shops
And well guarded by the cops.

The turquoise sea is really nice
And it has nooo price
The golden sand is divine
And the men are really fine.

The food is sooooo sweet
It is a lovely treat
The beer is really cheap
And the cars go *beep, beep*.

The coves are really lush
You can have a free slush
The white coves glow
Line some glistening snow.

It is not all year round
It only costs 700 pound
The hotel is really big
And sells raw pig.

My holiday is over
I am going back to Dover
This is the end of my roam
I am on my way home.

Tain Leavy (12)
Kingsbury School & Sports College, Erdington

Fairytale Flowers

It's where the lilies grow,
a place you may not know,
flowers here and flowers there,
the scent of flowers everywhere.

As we walk along the stream,
It's truly real, not a dream,
stop, wait and take a look,
it's like a fairy tale in a book.

The sunshine gleams through the trees,
leaves are carried in the breeze,
it makes you smile the way it gleams,
but when you're there thoughts
change to dreams.

Demileigh Collins (12)
Kingsbury School & Sports College, Erdington

I Would Love To Go To Spain

I would love to go to Spain
On a private aeroplane

When I'm there
I have to stare

At the sea
Gleaming back at me

All the Spanish food
To not try would be rude

You'll want to stay forever
In any kind of weather

You can see a beautiful sight
Every day and night

But when you have to go
Your sadness will show

To leave Spain
And go back to all the rain.

Danielle Harvey (12)
Kingsbury School & Sports College, Erdington

Seville

Seville,
My devil,
When the sun set low,
The night will glow,

Wanna explore Granada,
Search for Alhambra,
Swim in the shiny sapphire sea,
Oh just let me por favor

Tick-tock pass the time,
Let me try the finest wine,
Bring me there,
Bring me here

Seville,
My devil
Adios me Seville . . .

Nur Izzati Mohamad Hariri (13)
Kingsbury School & Sports College, Erdington

Untitled

I want to see Japan's rise and plunder,
To show its beauty in the light
I want to see all its wonders
In the day or in the night.

I need to ride on France's trains
And see its wondrous tower
See the Louvre again and again
Hour after hour!

I must see Egypt's ancient goats
And make it all worthwhile
I want to check on all the boats
And float up on the Nile!

I want to see the whole wide world,
And not miss any of it
They do say the Earth is my pearl
And I want to always have it!

Kelly Shale (12)
Kingsbury School & Sports College, Erdington

The Silent Walk

I went to the park
A dog barked
And a rat squeaked
But not a sound was heard

So I went to the zoo
A lion roared
And a monkey screamed
But not a sound was to be heard

So I went to the seaside
A ship went by
And a car drove by
But not a sound was to be heard

So I went to the swimming baths
A baby screamed
And the children laughed
But not a sound was to be heard

So I lived in a silent world.

Leanne Lowe (12)
Kingsbury School & Sports College, Erdington

I Wanna Go Somewhere . . .

I wanna go somewhere
Anywhere but here
I wanna go somewhere
That's not too near.

I wanna go somewhere
With warm hot days
I wanna go somewhere
With a nice place to stay.

I wanna go somewhere
That makes me feel at home
I wanna go somewhere
Where I can be alone.

I wanna go somewhere
With warm hot seas
I wanna go somewhere
Where I can be me.

I wanna go somewhere
Where I can have fun
I wanna go somewhere
Where I can lie in the sun.

I wanna go somewhere
Where can I go?
If you have any ideas
Please let me know.

Bethany Joesbury (12)
Kingsbury School & Sports College, Erdington

Me

As long as I live
I will always be
Myself - no one else
Only me.

Like a tree -
A shy tree, a willow
Not an oak
Big and strong.

I'd love to be an animal
A bird flying free,
Or a horse
Cantering is for me.

The future looks good,
I can't wait
I'll be an artist,
Or an author, writing and writing.

Danielle Pryor (11)
Kingsbury School & Sports College, Erdington

Me!

As long as I live
I shall always be
Myself - and no other
Just me!

Like a wave -
Fast and strong
From a beach or
Sea, and salty

Like a sound -
Moving around and
Giving sound waves to
Everyone.

Wanting to become a
DJ or a lawyer, live
My life without
Disasters!

Sakub Yasin (11)
Kingsbury School & Sports College, Erdington

Me

I'm me
and that's all I can be
just me.

Like a flower
petal, small
and round
silent, make
no sound

Like a tree
tall and
widow
old and
happy

Like a dog
lazy and sleepy
that's all I can
be me

I do not know
what I would be
all I know is that
I'm me

I'm me and that's all I can be
just me
me me me
that's all I can be
me.

Kimberley Buck (12)
Kingsbury School & Sports College, Erdington

United States Of America

U is for USA, a big and powerful country.
N is for never, they never back down to a war.
I is for Israel, they are at war with Israel.
T is for tiny, but they are not.
E is for every day, it's like war every day.
D is for dollars, they make lots of that.

S is for stars, which there are a lot of.
T is for time, will they have enough time?
A is for amazing, it's amazingly big.
T is for time, will I have enough time?
E is for everything, they always have that.
S is for Spears, Britney's last name.

O is for only, only I can make my choice.
F is for fame, lots and lots of fame!

A is for America, I want to live there.
M is for movies, I love American movies.
E is for every day, there's every day shopping.
R is for real life, real life things happen.
I is for idiots, there's a lot of idiots in USA.
C is for Cuba, an American island.
A is for America, I want to live there.

Charlotte Beirne (11)
Kingsbury School & Sports College, Erdington

In Me

As long as I live
I shall always be
Myself - and no other
Just me.

Like a flower
With super power
With straight hair
With always someone there.

I love the sun
All upon
And I have to
Have some fun.

In my future
I want a great culture
Being a hairdresser
This is for people as well in Manchester!

Leona Taylor (11)
Kingsbury School & Sports College, Erdington

This Is Me

As long as I live
I shall always be
myself - and no other
just me

Like an oak
tree, strong
and big
thick and tall

I'm a quad
bike strong
and fast
to bring a smile.

In the future
I would like to be
an emergency person
big, good, brave and strong.

Brett Bick (11)
Kingsbury School & Sports College, Erdington

My Life

As long as I live,
I will be happy,
never angry never snappy,
I am proud,

I stand with pride,
like a tree,
that stands to be counted,
that'll never hide,

God gave us a life to live proudly,
not too quiet, not too loudly,
make friends so somebody's there,
give of yourself always share,

I'll die like everyone else yes I'll die,
but I'll die proud and never cry,
I'll lay in my coffin with a smile on my face,
I'll be dead - I rest my case,
but my spirit will never leave my heart,
for as long as I live the spirit will never depart.

Aaron Lovell (11)
Kingsbury School & Sports College, Erdington

Going Home

I feel the sand below me,
It's slipping through my toes,
The sea is coming at me, swishing
As it goes.

I walk into the distance,
I can smell the fresh sea air,
The hotel's getting closer, but I
Don't seem to care.

My last day is tomorrow,
And now I start to think, I have to pack and leave my room,
And then have one last drink.
I wake up the next morning, ready for the day
I get my things into my car
And then I drive away.

Chloe-Anne Holmes (12)
Kingsbury School & Sports College, Erdington

I Want To See

Australia I want to see
It is the place for me
Have a look at kangaroos
And maybe play some didgeridoos

Italy I want to visit
See Venice and Rome
See waterways and the Coliseum
And maybe then go home

Maybe I'll have a peek at France
Eiffel Tower and all
Try the food and the wine
It will be a ball

I want to have a look at Brazil
Even though it's hot
I may not know much about it
But this will stop me, not

I want to visit theme parks
Have a party in Spain
Maybe go to the beach
I hope it doesn't rain.

Christopher Hickman (12)
Kingsbury School & Sports College, Erdington

Spain

On an aeroplane
I'm going to Spain
I'll go to the beach
I'll go in the sea
Then I'll get my hotel key
Oh look at me
I'm in Spain the wonderful city.

Paige Hunter (12)
Kingsbury School & Sports College, Erdington

Somewhere

I wanna go somewhere
I wanna see a grizzly bear
I could look up at the stars
Oh my I can see Mars

I wanna lie on the beach
Oh no a stupid leech
I'm gonna lie back
Now get into my sack
Oh my look at me
In this lovely city.

Joanna Parkes (12)
Kingsbury School & Sports College, Erdington

Love

Love
Something that makes you smile
Something that makes life worthwhile
Love

Love
Sometimes it can be fake
Sometimes end in heartbreak
Love.

Sophie Brown (14)
Kingsbury School & Sports College, Erdington

You're In Our Hearts Forever

The flowers have all withered
And the sky has now gone grey.
The sun has gone in for time
And we're no longer gay.

The tears fall like raindrops
As we visit your grave each day.
We wish for you to come back to us
But in Heaven you must stay.

Our love for you will never fade
And the memories won't fade too,
Just please watch over us
As every day we think of you.

Tears will still fall
And hearts will still ache,
But I know now
That you're in a better place.

So be there for us our angel
You're in our hearts that's true.
And remember this one thing please
That we all love you.

RIP Keilyn

Zoe Peters (14)
Kingsbury School & Sports College, Erdington

If Only I?

If I was happy,
I would let you know,
The smiles of joy,
Just like a toy,
You'll see for sure,
Just as long as I show you more,

If I was sad,
You'll be just as mad,
The drops of tears,
Will bring you fears,

Tears with a smile,
Just as long as a mile,
Might drop for a while,
Just as long as I'm in denial,

If I was happy as well as sad,
My dreams will be just as mad,

If only I could make you glad.

Sigourney Gerald (15)
Kingsbury School & Sports College, Erdington

The Weather

The weather is hot
The weather is cold
The weather is changing
As the weeks go by

The skies are cloudy
The skies are fair
The skies are changing
Everywhere

It is raining
It is snowing
It is windy
Warm breezes blowing

The days are foggy
The days are clear
The weather is changing
Throughout the year

Global warming?

Rochelle Johnson (15)
Kingsbury School & Sports College, Erdington

Two Deaths And A Broken Heart

Two families that are both the same
Share a feud from the other's name.
A street brawl and a royal punishment
Will this feud end with love's consent?
A Capulet party and a broken heart
Forms a new-found love at the very start.
Kept secret for a short amount of time
But their love is challenged because of a crime.
Banished and forbidden to see his love
She's pretending to be dead in the Capulet tomb.
Now hearing the news, he rushes to her side but he left too soon
Seeing her there he drinks poison till he is at peace
But she wakes up and sees him at peace
So she takes his dagger and stabs herself.
Once discovered, their families of wealth
End their feud that has lasted for centuries
So now Verona has lost her enemies.

Lauren Wilding (14)
Kingsbury School & Sports College, Erdington

Romeo And Juliet

A tale of two lovers,
Parted by hate,
At first enemies,
But then a wedding date.

Two deaths come along,
What will happen now?
Banishment and tragedy,
Split the lovers up once more.

A plan is created,
But causes the deaths of the two lovers,
Mourning and regret,
Two families reunited together.

Sarah Smart (14)
Kingsbury School & Sports College, Erdington

Winter's Thrall

Far above an old cold town,
Zigzagging pathways like cracked glass,
Stand out against the night,
Snow encrusted towers conceal,

A secret only she knows,

In a room so newly swept,
Dusty cobwebs gone,
Therein lies a-sleeping,

A poor kitchen maid,

She slumbers softly in the cold,
The creeping frost is taking hold,

Upon her graceful form,

Air turning to ice in lungs,
And breath condensing in crystal clouds,
Closed eyes misting in silver chill,

Oh, who can save her from the cold?

The wild wind whistles through the eaves,
And howling spirits seek by night,
Cold forms to feed upon,

Oh, what can save her from the cold?

Icy chill in silenced springs,
Spreading like the plague,

Oh, what can save her from the cold?

Slow from peaceful slumber wakens she,
Rising like the dawn,
The sun to burn away the frost,
Upon this summer morn,

She lights the fire in the grate,
And stokes new life unto the flames,
And summer has her will.

Adam Pietrzak (14)
Kingsbury School & Sports College, Erdington

Romeo And Juliet

R omeo and Juliet a story of hate, conflict, tragedy and love
O n the city of Verona is where the story is set
M ontague has an ancient feud with Capulet
E ager to meet Rosaline, Juliet is who his heart falls for
O ver a couple of days the lovers get married to share their
love for evermore

A few murders, suicides, and fights occur in this Shakespearean
play
N ow when Tybalt kills Mercutio, on the ground where he lay
D esire for revenge rushes through Romeo and kills Juliet's
cousin on his wedding day

J uliet is forced to marry Paris who her father insisted on
U nfortunately Romeo was who she wanted to see
L awrence, the Friar, had a cunning plan to set them free
I n the end nothing goes according to plan and the letter does not
reach Romeo
E ventually this sad story ends by Juliet taking her life but first,
does Romeo
'T here never was a story of more woe
than that of Juliet and her Romeo.'

Hasan Mahmood (14)
Kingsbury School & Sports College, Erdington

Hard Times

Fate works in funny ways,
Everything in your life is going well
And then in a matter of hours
Your whole world can become a living hell.

It lingers in the back of everyone's mind
Some people think about it a lot.
Then when it happens to someone we know,
We all respond differently whether we like it or not.

Some fill with anger
And rage builds in their head.
Others are filled with sadness
And wish it were them instead.

Some people try to stop it happening
In any way they can.
Some people accept it,
Some don't give a damn.

It's a difficult time for everyone,
You're a jittery, muddled mess.
Falling in love is never easy
But we have to try our best.

Sophie Cox (14)
Kingsbury School & Sports College, Erdington

Drayton Manor

The day I went there,
I wouldn't call it nice,
It was raining half the day,
I sat there rolling dice.

Went on Stormforce 10,
Bounced out of my seat,
My picture came out really funny,
After. . . You should have seen my feet.

Got scared on Pandamonium,
The silver belt came off,
So glad that never happened to the harness,
There was no time to have a strop.

But all together,
It was fun,
Though it would have been better,
If there was some sun!

Pooja Gill (12)
Kingsbury School & Sports College, Erdington

My Mom

My mom is the tropical sea
always calm and never
rough. She always feels
like a brand new sofa
comfy and pleasant. She is
the tastiest thing you
could ever ask for. My
mom is the world, massive
in just one thin figure.

Reece Weston (11)
Kingsbury School & Sports College, Erdington

The Army

The general may shout, scream and moan,
And sometimes gets right up my nose.
A pain the neck,
Is what you could say.

When marching we're treated like pack horses,
Break a leg he says.
We run like cheetahs in the wild,
Doing as we are told.

Our journey finally comes to an end,
We all collapse like wilting plants.
Then sleep so deep,
As If we we're trying to reach the ocean floor.

Gunshots are heard,
They pierce our ears like knives.
Somebody yells,
We run to the spot where they lay.

The have already reached the seabed.

Ruth Dixon (12)
Kingsbury School & Sports College, Erdington

Megan Lucy Beckley That's My Name!

M is for mischievous which I can be
E is for an excellent student which I think I am
G is for generous that I am
A is for amazing that's the Beckleys!
N is for nice, I am nice.

L is for laughing which I do a lot
U is for unique I am unique
C is for caring, that's me!
Y is for Year 7 the year I am in

B is for boring I'm no way boring
E is for effort I always do my best
C is for clever, I'm a bit clever
K is for kid I am a kid
L is for loving I am very loving
E is for eleven that's my age
Y is for young, which I am.

Megan Beckley (11)
Kingsbury School & Sports College, Erdington

Egyptian Senses

I want to see a pyramid
built up very high
I would never ever think of it
built up to the sky.

I want to feel the sand
twinkle through my toes
feel the nice Egyptian breeze
flutter through my nose

I want to hear the River Nile
feel the fur of Egyptian goats
and make it worthwhile
and float on the ancient boats

I want to smell perfume
and sit outside at night
and see the stars and the moon
which would be shining very bright.

Sadé Robinson (12)
Kingsbury School & Sports College, Erdington

Asperger's Syndrome

A is for Asperger's Syndrome this appears on the autistic spectrum
S is for struggling because of the condition
P is for people that don't understand
E is for emotions we don't understand
R is for routine we crave so much
G is for geeks which bullies usually call us
E is for extra effort we need to put into our work
R is for rugby a sport which some people find hard
S is for SULP which is a big help

S is for senses that can be a trouble
Y is for yelling we hate so much
N is for noise which people who are autistic cannot stand
D is for difficult tasks or questions autistic people come across every day
R is for rules that must be followed
O is for open-minded people that autistic people find hard to interpret
M is for motor skills which can be affected
E is for everyone with Asperger's Syndrome.

Matthew Cross (13)
Kingsbury School & Sports College, Erdington

Romeo And Juliet

For never was there a tale of more woe
Than of Juliet and her Romeo
Where there is a brawl and many a fight
Where the prince arrives to put it right
Escalus acts as the high court judge
And tries to bury this ancient grudge.

Friar Lawrence is in on the plan
To make Romeo a happily married man
Two crazy teenagers from different worlds
A foolish boy and a confused girl
Who meet each other, and are married next day
Joined in holy matrimony in a rash way.

Two feuding families, Montague and Capulet
Who can't find it in themselves to bury the hatchet
Two star-crossed lovers who loved each other
Take their lives for one another
For never was there a tale of more woe
Than of Juliet and her Romeo.

Davaine Whyte (15)
Kingsbury School & Sports College, Erdington

I Love Being A Student

I love being a student,
at Kingsbury school,
it makes me happy,
and good galore.

I love being a student,
at Kingsbury school,
my tutors have smiles,
and make me laugh.

I love being a student,
at Kingsbury school,
even though maths,
and English is a bore.

I love being a student,
at Kingsbury school,
break time and lunchtime,
is best of all.

I love being a student,
at Kingsbury school,
Fridays are a blast,
home time at last.

Jennifer Horspool (11)
Kingsbury School & Sports College, Erdington

Ice Cream Is . . .

Ice cream is yummy, yummy for my tummy.
Ice cream, ice cream, we all scream for ice cream!
The ice cream van gets stuck in muck,
I was in my room reading a book,
When I heard a tune playing, I had a look.
Yey! It was the ice cream van!
Ice cream, ice cream, we all scream for ice cream!
The ice cream man's name is Owen,
Goodbye, goodbye, it's the end of my poem!

Bethany Wignall (11)
Kingsbury School & Sports College, Erdington

Detention

In my English class
I didn't pay attention
So the teacher gave me a detention

As my detention came near
My head was full of fear
The children were quiet, as I walked in you couldn't even
Hear the drop of a pin.

The teacher gave me a hundred lines
I was told they had to be written clearly and fine
The clock was ticking, as I looked around I could see
All the other pupils' pencils flicking.

The end came for my detention
It taught me to pay more attention.

Talia Ali (11)
Kingsbury School & Sports College, Erdington

Charlie-Shauna Wager

C is for cheeky, I love being cheeky
H is for honest, I'm always honest
A is for athletic, I adore athletics
R is for real, I'm real not fake
L is for love, I'm good at showing love
I is for I-Tunes, I always listen to them
E is for extreme, extreme is defo me.

S is for star, o yeah I am a star!
H is for happy, because I'm always happy
A is for angel, an angel with attitude
U is for unique, unique is definitely me
N is for naughty, I put the N in naughty
A is for annoying, which I can be.

W is for wager derr it's my name!
A is for amazing, erm get a life if you're amazing what am I?
G is for gorgeous, because I am.
E is for excited, calm down it is only a poem.
R is for R'N'B, I'm just the R'N'B queen.

Charlie-Shauna Wager (12)
Kingsbury School & Sports College, Erdington

Excuses!

Sorry I didn't do my homework Sir
because my hamster died.

Sorry I didn't do my homework Sir
because my cousin is going deaf and blind.

Sorry I didn't do my homework Sir
banged my head and the doctor
diagnosed me and thought I was dead.

That's enough what a load
of excuses!

No Sir it's true I promise it's true!

Jordan Lovell (11)
Kingsbury School & Sports College, Erdington

So Called Friend

I sit hoping you notice me.
You're meant to be a mate but you leave me.
Why don't you see me?
I'm not invisible!
I start to cry
Then you notice me,
'Are you ok?' You ask
I reply with a simple lie,
'You're my problem!' my head shouts.
I just want you to be a friend all the time
Not when you want to be.

Gemma Johnson (15)
Kingsbury School & Sports College, Erdington

What I Saw In You

Sometimes I stop and wonder
About what I saw in you,
Was it in your eyes
Or the things you used to do?

It was that first time I saw you,
The first time that we met,
The way I laid eyes on you
Oh how could I forget?

My friends thought I was crazy
It was love at first sight,
My heart lead me to believe
That you were Mr Right.

He said he wanted to talk
He wanted to give us a try!
But how was I to know
That that was all a lie?

We went out for while
Everything was great,
But then there was a rumour
And my love turned into hate.

I heard if from a friend
The rumour, it was true!
How you couldn't be honest
And tell me we were through!

How was I so stupid?
Why couldn't I see?
We weren't right together
We just weren't meant to be.

But you and I are over
You and I are through,
This brings be back to the question
About what I saw in you?

Helena Borthwick (14)
Kingsbury School & Sports College, Erdington

Fear

I feel the fear,
When they come near,
I am scared
My heart begins to pound.

As I walk down the corridor,
I pretend to walk into a door,
They always hurt me
I don't know what to do.

My heart races,
As I see those familiar faces,
All spinning round my head,
I think I'm going to faint.

I am alone and frightened,
As the rope is being tightened,
I don't know what to do,
Please, help me!

Claire Griffiths (14)
Kingsbury School & Sports College, Erdington

Being Black

Being black hurts
Even worse if you speak first
Can't walk the street without being scared
Cos someone might 'Shank you' and leave you for dead
Black History Month only comes once a year
But the kids in school don't really give a care
It's their lack of knowledge of the homeland
All they wanna know bout is 'Gangs'
But soon enough they'll realise
To get anywhere in life they need to open their eyes
And see the reality of the world
You've got to have a good education if you wanna buy all
Those diamonds and pearls!

Kalesha Palmer (14)
Kingsbury School & Sports College, Erdington

Excuse.A

Hi, my name is Excuse, Excuse always. Fine it isn't my name, I have a
boring name wait for it . . . it's Mary, Mary Always; Honest Always is the
family name. Like give me a problem and bam-bam I have an answer.
Sorry, about that I'm bored you see, got stuck in 'ere for making
excuses. I know what I'll do to get out I'll make an excuse.
Tomorrow morning's excuse. . .
Sorry Miss I'm late.
Don't shout at me yet
I've got an excuse
You'll never believe what happened to me,
Teacher says, 'Here we go again,'
Sorry Miss, I went to Mars,
To count one by one all the stars.
And guess what the bus was late;
It'll be 9.20 at this rate
My dad just came home from Japan,
To tell you what he had quite a tan
I'm quite appalled a train doesn't stop here
Oh, please let me go home I'm feeling quite queer
The air balloon burst, I was in France
Oh gosh I've got ants in my pants,
To tell you the truth, I wanted to skydive
Thank goodness I landed, in Cape Town *alive*
Round in my boat, with sausage and eggy
I'm feeling so fine, the boat's going steady
Scotland I'm at now, reaching for Wales
Jennifer's rowing quite hard on those sails
At last I've reached England, oh this is taking long
By the time I get there you'll all be gone.

So that's what happened to me, sorry I'm late
But next time I want to go to the United States.

Jadine Ijoyah (11)
Kingsbury School & Sports College, Erdington

What Can I See All Around Me . . .

What can I see all around me
I can see the bees
I can see the trees
And bless me I just sneezed
All these things happen to me in the summer

What can I see all around me
I can see myself breathe
I can see and smell the leaves
But what do I believe
All these things happen to me in the autumn

What can I see all around me
I can see the snow
As I go with the flow
But I tie my scarf as I go
All these things happen to me in the winter

What can I see all around me
I can see a flower
I can see I have the power
But after I need to cool down with a shower
All these things happen to me during a springtime exam.

Lakvinder Kaur (12)
Ninestiles Technology College, Acocks Green

Different People

We are all very different people, all unique and special in our own way,
Wide ranges of stories, opinions and thoughts we all have different
things to say.
Our size, our image, our looks, our skin colours too,
Everyone's an individual, you and me too!
Favourite colours, interesting facts, so many walks of life,
Fantastic food by different people used with a fork and knife.
Human intelligence, beauty and brains within everyone's hearts
and soul.
Pounding, beating in everyone like a gallop of a foal.
So take a chance, meet new people and tell them aloud,
'I'm different, special and unique and for this I'm very proud.'

Whitney Donaldson (11)
Ninestiles Technology College, Acocks Green

The Things That Happen In Books

I love reading
I love vampires bleeding
I love fairies flying
I love little girls crying

I love horrible teens
And movie scenes
I love good friends
And happy ends

I love moms
And detonation bombs
I love dirty muck
And a crook

I love a good book
Oh I love a good book

I love reading
I love vampires bleeding
I love fairies flying
I love little girls crying.

Amy Boland (11)
Ninestiles Technology College, Acocks Green

School!

School rocks,
Let's rock 'n' roll,
School's out,
Let's dance about.

Went to class,
Didn't bring my books,
All the teachers are
Giving me dirty looks.

Dancing in the hall,
Doing the hustle,
And one of the teachers,
Was showing me her muscles.

Gurpreet Rathore (12)
Ninestiles Technology College, Acocks Green

Seasons

Spring, summer, autumn, winter,
Every year they are different,
The seasons are always changing,
Each and every single year.

Spring is when baby animals are born,
When fluorescent butterflies fly across your lawn,
Lots of pretty coloured flowers poke their dainty heads,
Out of the snow-covered flower beds.

Summer is when you go with your family to the beach,
Having lots of fun and enjoying the sun,
You can go to the fair with your friends,
And you wish the day would never end.

Autumn is the season of care and giving,
Providing for the homeless and hungry,
The farmers begin to harvest their crops,
And everyone starts wearing warm, cozy jumpers and long-sleeved tops.

'Tis the season to be jolly,
The month of advent leading to the birth of Jesus Christ,
Giving presents and making merry,
Looking forward to a new year and a new start.

Spring, summer, autumn, winter,
Every year they are different,
The seasons are always changing,
Each and every single year.

Elizabeth Gould (12)
Ninestiles Technology College, Acocks Green

Not About The Rain!

Four wheels, four seasons!
Spring, summer, autumn, winter
Sands turn in the hours
Time stands still!

I sit and watch the rain from my windows
Seeing nothing within those
Except my reflection on the glass
Any other details I pass,
Over I am thinking of the rain!
I plunge down rather deep
Only ecstasy helps me sleep
I am my own repression!

This rain is thick it's blinding me
Nothing more, I cannot see
If it continues raining there'll be a flood!

Madeleine Levy (16)
Ninestiles Technology College, Acocks Green

Love Poem

When we first met,
You made me smile.
With your lovely cute face,
You're so ace.

As we walked down the road,
Hand in hand.
You looked at me,
I'm in love maybe.

You made me smile,
You made me cry.
I felt like I could fly,
Up into the sky.

You and me,
As happy as can be.
Together whenever,
Together forever.

When we're apart,
I feel so sad.
I'll be thinking of you,
If only you knew.

So hold my hand,
Don't let go.
Remember you will always have a special place,
Right here in my heart!

Laura Brinkworth (13)
Ninestiles Technology College, Acocks Green

Then She Was Gone

You would see her shadow moving
And every sound she made.
You would hear her heart pump louder
But then she would just fade.

You would hear her voice grow louder
And this is what you'd fear
You'd see her smash the windows
And then she'd disappear.

You'd see her run through corridors
And switch all the lights on
She would run towards the kitchen
And then she was gone.

Aishah Mahmood (13)
Ninestiles Technology College, Acocks Green

I'm Sorry

I'm sorry for all the hurt,
And all the pain,
It does hurt your feelings
Now that is sane.

But if you say sorry,
Does it last?
I would like to turn back time,
And change the past.

I know it's impossible,
But I will try,
To hold my feelings,
And do not cry.

I am sorry,
Please forgive me,
I can now admit,
I can really now see.

That in your head
It is a mixed up mind
So now I will try
I'll be friendly and kind.

We may be friends
I see it now
So if you won't
I can be your pal.

Stacie Hughes (13)
Ninestiles Technology College, Acocks Green

Would You Make A Difference?

If you could see through someone else's eyes,
If you could see all the love and lies,
If you could be someone else for the day,
Like Tony Blair what would you say?
Would you try to make the difference?

If you walk through someone's dreams,
If you could be in one of them teams,
If you could stop poverty and cancer,
If you could be the one chancer,
Would you try to make the difference.

If you could do something,
In one single tiny blink
If you were the pacific seas,
If you was a massive breeze,
Would you make the difference?

Rachel Hanrahan (13)
Ninestiles Technology College, Acocks Green

Through The Eyes Of. . .

When you're at home,
Safe in your bed,
Give a quick thought,
For the homeless instead.

He has little food,
His name is the street,
He is the person,
Who we don't want to meet.

Cold and starving,
Nobody cares,
No money no hope,
Rags he wears.

Amie Spencer (14)
Oldbury College of Sport, Oldbury

I Am

I am myself nobody else
Nobody can change me because I am myself
I do not copy anyone's style or answers
I am myself
No one can tell me what to wear or what music to listen to
I am myself
I like what I like, no one can tell me what I should like
I am myself
If I want to spend all my money at once no one can stop me
I am myself
No one can tell what to eat and drink
I am myself
No one can tell me what job I should do
I am myself
No one can tell me who I should like, I like who I like
I am myself!

Alex Wood (12)
Oldbury College of Sport, Oldbury

A Robin's Day

In wintertime they come out most
flying around landing on posts.
Collecting twigs,
With his small legs,
So he can cover his eggs.

Their nest is small,
But very tall.
In a big oak tree,
Where the children climb,
They race away, but have very little time.

So they flap away,
And then they say,
Tweet, tweet and goodbye!
They return to their nest,
So they can rest.
Then that way,
They can come out to play, another day.

Jason Booth (11)
Oldbury College of Sport, Oldbury

Is There Really A God?

The grass is green, the sky is blue
I can see everything except for you.
The night is dark,
The day is bright,
You see everything even in the night.

You hear all I hear some,
But you see all even people
Who have broken the law.
But still people think that
You don't exist. I don't
Think they realise you made
Them like this.

He knows all things that
Happen, but still people
Complain about things that
Don't matter. This is why
People ask is there
Really a God?

Raekwon Douglas (12)
Oldbury College of Sport, Oldbury

You'll Be Fine

My life is perfect, except for one thing
It started out small, but then began to grow
I used to dance when I was happy, now I get upset and I only sing
Don't leave us here, don't you see the fear in our tears
Your heart will heal, or we hope it does
Oh dear brother don't go, you'll stay here and we'll love you so
The flowers bloom, the sky is blue
Live your life like you want to, don't listen to others who tell you what to do
Your beat is low, don't mean you have to go slow
If you're calm, you'll be fine
Don't say nothing you don't want to say
Don't lie, just tell the truth
Get on with your life, the way you want to because it's your choice

Years go by without a sound, you're better and you hear the pound
Of your heart, you're back to the start
Don't worry now, you're fine, your heartbeat's so right
You'll live the way you've always wanted to
You can do anything, just see what your life will bring.

Ellouise Wheelwright (11)
Oldbury College of Sport, Oldbury

The Whizzing Car!

There's a car who whizzes down my road.
With its engine flying!
I can only hear pump, pump like a fly.
He bibs his horn like a telephone rattling by.
He's sparkling car zooms done on a rough surface.
He swerves to swerve like a roller-coaster toy.
There's a cat who runs into the road and tries to pump like a fly.
The sparkly car roars along with his engine by.
This car goes faster than a roller coaster.
He nearly goes into a winter tree.
He stops his car at the bottom of the road and checks his front.
His car's like a mouth as it whizzes by.
He looks like a rally driver on a track.
He looks like his engine's gonna fall off.

Leah Ainge (12)
Oldbury College of Sport, Oldbury

My Life As A Flower

I am a pretty flower,
I live in gardens,
and I sometimes swish in the wind
die in winter,
but I come back in spring,
people buy me as presents for people
and put us in water so we can drink
when winter comes it gets cold,
it freezes and I want to run home
when it gets hot in the park
people pick me,
damage my petals
and my stem.
I die of thirst
and hunger
I hate the rain,
how it thunders down,
it makes me sad
so I could run away
and shelter under a tree,
and that's my life as a flower!

Alice Rowley (12)
Oldbury College of Sport, Oldbury

Who Am I?

My leaves are as green as grass,
My branches are never straight,
My feet are deep into the ground,
My body is always cut down for paper,
My leaves and branches can be made into a house,
My branches are like a nest,
My branches have beehives hanging down,
And my height can be small or tall.

Bears climb up me to get honey out of the hives,
My body never stops growing until my feet are into the ground,
My leaves fall off,
And my leaves grow back again,
You can find me in parks,
Or you can find me near lakes,
You can find me on grass,
Or you can find me near grass.
Do you know who I am?
Yes, I'm a tree.

Rebekah Massy (12)
Oldbury College of Sport, Oldbury

Homework!

Homework is like a snake
Pulling me away from my free time
Homework is like a hippo strong and dangerous
Destroying my time of fun
Homework is like a cat
Waiting for you on the mat
Homework is like old folk
It's so hard it makes me choke
Homework is like an owl
Asleep until you forget it

Homework is like a magician
Full of surprises and evil tricks
Homework is like a huge fire
Burning and painful
Homework is long and hard
As a double-decker bus
Homework is like a monster
Eating your brains out
Homework is like a puppy all cute and cuddly
But when come to do it's mean and vicious
Homework is like a torture chamber
Until you come to do it then you meet your doom
But in the end all the pain and suffering
Was just a bad dream.

Lyle Farnell (12)
Oldbury College of Sport, Oldbury

Butterflies

Up high it zooms
Her wings bloom
So beautiful it's something you would love to see
Or even something you would love to be
Up high it zooms
Her wings bloom
You'll see her in the day
So pretty you'll have nothing to say
Up high it zooms
Her wings bloom
She could be anywhere
And when you see her you'll really care
Up high it zooms her wings bloom
And don't forget to this someone you've never met
When you're going bye don't forget to say hi!
Up high it zooms her wings bloom
Butterflies, butterflies all around
Never ever touching the ground
Up high it zooms her wings bloom
It flies in the sky on her wings patterns lie
Goodbye, goodbye little butterfly.

Leena Sharma (12)
Oldbury College of Sport, Oldbury

Chocolate

Milky chocolate and so sweet,
So wonderfully divine for me to eat!
Creamy white chocolate melting in my mouth,
I wish I could fill it all over my house!
I wish I could make a universe made of chocolate,
Even the coffees would taste of mocha!
Wish I could build a chocolate factory all to myself,
It would be all mine - not for anyone else!
I ate so much chocolate - I look like a pig!
Oh my gosh look at my stomach, it looks so big!

Lamis Amireh (11)
Oldbury College of Sport, Oldbury

Sammy The Sheepdog

Chasing sheep is what I do,
I'm scared of the big ones that go 'Moo.'

My name is Sammy and I'm a dog,
Mostly I chase them in the fog.

I love my job it's really swell,
Most important, I do it well.

My owner lets them out the pen.
I run real fast right out my den.

Silly sheep they really are,
In looks I win for sure, by far.

I'm only one, I turned last night,
Of course I win in all the fights.

I'm a big dog, I don't cry,
I'm going to go play so here's goodbye.

Sofia Butt (14)
Oldbury College of Sport, Oldbury

Shopping

It's what every woman needs to do
Shop their Saturdays all way through.
Pink, purple even black which colour bag
Should I have?
Skinny jeans, bootleg, normal fit which one
Should I have to wear for a drink?
Strappy, boobtube, backless which one should
I choose for my next shopping trip?
High heels, wedges which one should I
Pick for the sake of it?
Halterneck, neckless which one should I
Choose to win best dressed?
Now the day's all done,
I wish I could carry on,
But now you know the true
Meaning of a woman's life.

Laura Wilcox (13)
Oldbury College of Sport, Oldbury

Be Who You Are Not Anyone Else!

I know you can't speak
But you can give me a smile
It makes me feel bad
When you're looking sad.

You can't say a word
So you won't be heard
I am always here
So don't have fear.

I like it the way you are
You're like my shining star.

Olivia Wright (14)
Oldbury College of Sport, Oldbury

The World

I see this world is very beautiful,
I see this world full of war.
I see this world is full of excitement and love,
I see this world full of hate and despair.

As beautiful as love,
As ugly as hate,
But why can't the world be a lovely place?

So if I look at the world in your eyes,
And you look from mine,
Yours will be wild and wacky,
But so will mine.
But if we look in someone else's,
You will see fear, sadness and loneliness.

So everyone should see the world not as a fearless place,
But as a happy, joyful place.

But I can't tell you why.

Sabrina Kumari (12)
Oldbury College of Sport, Oldbury

The World

Why, why are we here?
What is the meaning of the Big Bang
The death of a little star.
Brought so much life
Is the meaning to love and not hate
It is us then why is there so much hate
Maybe it is to live
Then why is there so much death?
Life started with the death of a little star
And soon will end with another death of a star
Maybe the meaning is to die
What do you think?

Paul Hughes (13)
Oldbury College of Sport, Oldbury

The Meaning Of Life: Why Are We Here?

We are here to serve a purpose
To live
We enjoy our lives in any way possible
To live
We should be able to get along so it's possible
To live
You see on the news children dying not having a chance
To live
Christians, Muslims, Sikhs, Jehovah's Witnesses, Hindus believe
you should live
The meaning of life is to live it not to fall short of it
When we are children, we learn and we laugh and we live
We were part of His planet millions of years ago
For millions of years we have lived, not died
You see in the news people dying
If we are meant to die when we are old and have lived
The meaning of life is to live!

Jordan Gibbs (12)
Oldbury College of Sport, Oldbury

I Cared!

Even though I didn't go
I cared.
Even though I didn't cry
I cared.
Even though I didn't tell anyone
I cared.
Even though nobody knew
I cared.
I know she is in a better place
I cared.

Megan Hill (12)
Oldbury College of Sport, Oldbury

As Far As I Know . . .

You are as tall as a skyscraper,
But as small as a mouse.
You are as wide as the universe,
But as thin as thin can be.

As far as I know,
It doesn't really matter,
How tall, small, wide or thin
You are.

You are who you are,
No more, no less.
You can only do
Your best.

Amanda Sears (12)
Oldbury College of Sport, Oldbury

My Poem

This is my poem from start to finish,
Everyone listen so you can tell that the bell is ringing.
So gather round,
And get your dogs and cats from the pound.
So
Stop that fighting,
And prepare for some lightning
Cause we're going from town to town.
Are you ready, get steady.
Because
This is my poem,
Get flown!

Beth Chantler (13)
Oldbury College of Sport, Oldbury

What Is The Meaning Of Life?

Why are we here, put on this Earth?
Is it to make each other's lives a worth?

Do we have a certain meaning?
Or sometimes is it just a feeling?

Does life have a certain purpose?
Or is it like one big circus?

Is our life set in a particular direction?
Or is it a set of random selections?

Gurpreet Ghuman (12)
Oldbury College of Sport, Oldbury

My Life As Vermin!

My life is hell,
I'm not treated well.

I'm a rat,
But I'd rather be eaten by a cat.

I suffer night and day,
It's not like I can have my say.

Those sharp pointy pricks,
Oh the pain really sticks.

It won't be long before,
They say goodnight and close the door.

Rebecca Pearsall (11)
Oldbury College of Sport, Oldbury

I Am A Dog

I am a dog,
I chased a frog,
I went to Spain,
Then got on a plane,
If I could, I'd say,
I've come to play.

When I came back,
I saw a black cat,
Her name was Socks,
She sleeps in a box,
I saw JoJo,
And he drank my cocoa.

So I'm here to say,
I love you every day.

I am a dog.

Ashleigh Barratt (11)
Oldbury College of Sport, Oldbury

Pandora - My Turn!

Oh finally!

I'm in the limelight, I'm allowed
to talk, I'm a cute, fluffy panda
with eyes like a hawk.

You'd never believe it but I'm a
pencil case.
and pick up some pace.

There's a dopey dude called Matthew P
who'd go and stick pencils in me.

So one day, I taught him a lesson,
when Sadie whacked him with me,
and my work was done.

So now that Matthew's reign of
terror is done, he will never go sticking
pens in my bum!

Sadie Redding (13)
Oldbury College of Sport, Oldbury

What Am I?

They are things of pleasure,
Whatever the weather.
Shapes and sizes,
Full of surprises.
Pink or blue
Any colour will do
It is a thing of beauty
And it has a duty
To make a garden look lovely
Nice and snuggly

But just 1 question
for you to make a suggestion

What am I?
Don't be scared no need to cover
because I am a beautiful flower.

Jasmyn Williams (11)
Oldbury College of Sport, Oldbury

What Is The Meaning Of Life?

What is the meaning of life?
We wake up, we go to school.
Then we go to sleep
Why are we on this Earth?
Is it because God had to make us,
Why, oh why
Do people die?
Who knows where people
Go when they die
Why do people hate their life?

Amy Spence (13)
Oldbury College of Sport, Oldbury

A Lost Soul

Down in these trenches
We're soldiers at war
Fighting for a cause
That seems lost

We're in a world of monsters
In a world of war
Thoughts of home
Keep us going

I'm lucky I'm alive
I savour each breath
As it may be my last
We savour each sensation of cold, violent touch

Not so lucky
Is one lost soul
Who fought three years for this cause
The violent mist knocked him down
His hands so cold he couldn't reach his mask in time.

Appeared in his lungs an ocean
Drowning him at sea
His soul still wonders on
I feel his presence
When I stand ready to fight his heartless murders.

There was no ceremony for his soul
The vicar was busy at present
His soul has gone away from here
His soul is lost at sea.

Gemma White (14)
Oldbury College of Sport, Oldbury

Life

Life is good,
Life is great,
It is filled with unfilled fate,
Life was given to be lived right,
Use it well through day and night,
Your childhood should be filled with greatness,
Give it 100 percent and
No more less!
So remember this poem for the rest of your
Life, and don't get using
A stupid knife.

Sophie Powell (13)
Oldbury College of Sport, Oldbury

Happy Moments

When I am in a bad mood
or I am sad, or when there is
no one to cheer me up, I don't
try to stay sad for the rest of
the day. Looking like a saddo
who has no one in the world.

So I sit down on the couch
put in the TV, get something
to chew or eat and go on,
happy, wonderful joy riding to
what I call the 'Happy moments.'

After a while I will put this great
big smile on my face as if it
is Christmas Day.

So if you are feeling sad for
yourself or in a bad mood, don't
just sit there, take my advice
go on a happy, wonderful
joy riding to 'Happy moments!'

Belise Nirin Giyimana (13)
Oldbury College of Sport, Oldbury

Why Are We Here?

Why are we here?
I don't know.

Maybe we are here,
Too look after each other!

But with all this love and hate,
No one classes each other as their mate.

Why is everyone always fighting?
I don't know but it's very frightening.

Why can't everyone love each other?
For what they are and what they do.

Why are we here?
I still don't know.

But when I find out,
I will let you know!

Gemma Giles (14)
Oldbury College of Sport, Oldbury

The Good Times

The good times are memories that are with you forever.
They are there like the treasures you keep in a box.
Except they are in your heart and you can't lose them.
When I'm sad and lonely I think of the good times and
get over my gloomy phase.
They make me blissful and joyful, because I know
there is nothing bad about them.
I can feel my heart getting bigger and bigger, and not
getting broken from the bad memories.
The bad weather makes me think about the good times
which makes me feel nice and bright.
The world is a place where lots of things will take
place, they should all be good but we need to make that happen.

Bethany Littleton (12)
Oldbury College of Sport, Oldbury

The Earth

Find the Earth,
The place for birth.
All of UK Towns,
The Queen always crowns,
All the countries there can be,
All of them you will see,
In your lesson of geography,
Spain, China, Russia and Japan.
All of these countries can dance,
All can be very nasty,
But everyone is lucky,
Even them little duckies,
We lose some, we gain some,
None of us are that dumb,
So please respect our Earth,
So please don't do graffiti on the turf
God is here, here in the place called Earth!

Aaron Randhawa (12)
Oldbury College of Sport, Oldbury

I Would

If I could change something that has happened.
You know, stop it from happening to begin with.
I would warn people about earthquakes and tornados.
I would warn people about poverty and illness.
I would warn people about drugs, joyriding and guns.
But if I was selfish, you know the kind.
Who would go back in time to copy homework,
Who would take advantage of the situation.
Just imagine if this happened,
Would I still be here? Would you still be here?
Maybe we would all be happy?

Leah Elsworth (12)
Oldbury College of Sport, Oldbury

If I Could Turn Back Time

Friday 13th February 2003,
was when she died.
How could this be?
O why did she die?

My nan was the poor unlucky soul,
who lost her life on that day.
She was cut short by cancer,
much to my family's dismay.

Friday 13th February 2003,
was when she died,
How could this be?
O why did she die?

If I could turn back time,
my nan would not have died.
If we could turn back time,
we could be as before.

If you could turn back time,
Is there anything you would change?

Kierron Barker (12)
Oldbury College of Sport, Oldbury

Time Turn

Turn back time what would you change?
The way you were to family and friends?
Would you treat the world with better care?
Would you show people how to share?

Time is a thing not to be wasted,
Like a food you've never tasted,
If you never take a risk,
You will never know,
How things will go.

To turn back time I could see,
How things were or will be,
People who died,
People who cried,
Over war and peace.
Black and white we are all the same.
Turn back time what would you change?

Abbie-Leigh Allard (13)
Oldbury College of Sport, Oldbury

I Send This Message

I send this message to every one
Who has had sorrow inside and lost someone
I know how you feel
I know that you're hurt
So stop the crying
And it's time to insert
The happiness, the joy, the cries of laughter
And that's the way I survived after,
So remember you're intelligent kid,
Remember what I did.

I send this message
To everyone
Who has had sorrow inside
And lost someone
I know how you feel
I know that you're hurt
So stop the tears
And it's time to be alert
To the happiness, the joy
The cries of laughter
And that's the way
I survived after,
So remember
You're intelligent kid,
Remember what I did
Remember,
What I did!

Kieron Cherrington (12)
Oldbury College of Sport, Oldbury

Why Are We Here?

Why are we here?
May God knows.

The meaning of life
Maybe to live and learn.

The biggest truth of life
Maybe death.

Good times, great memories
Why don't you share.

Why is there hate and cruelness everywhere?

Why is the world so upset?

Time is short and
You haven't done a lot.

So come on get up, go out
And teach this world to love and share.

Kirandeep Kaur (13)
Oldbury College of Sport, Oldbury

Untitled

Another day, another night,
Another day, another fight,
Men's hearts hammering,
Men's guns stammering,
Fight at the home of the broken,
The fight for freedom lives on,
When will the darkness turn to light?
Will it end tonight?
Is the end nigh?
The rains come hard and fast,
The planes overhead thunder and boom,
The deafening blasts,
With aches and pains and wailing galore,
Guns blaze more and more,
Will it stop?
Will it cease?
The only thing to reassure,
Is the hope that you might just make it.

Amrit Kaur (13)
Perryfields High School, Oldbury

People Have Feelings

People have feelings, boys and girls too
I have feelings just like you
No one thinks when they call you names,
You say sticks and stones and they play games.
Teachers say stuff to make you feel better,
But really who's having the pleasure.
You have this one person who picks
On you the most.
Makes you feel horrible, ugly and lost.
Parents say it's because they love you.

Ignore the person and they'll go away.
But the next thing you know they're in your face.
Walk away as they all say but there's
Always that one special day.
That one day when you stand up for yourself.
Use abuse back and a fight breaks out.
A punch in the stomach ow, not fair.

You've had enough now,
And today is your last row
For tomorrow I won't be here
Because I've disappeared
All because of my peer.

Ashleigh Simpson (13)
Perryfields High School, Oldbury

Toys

My toys come alive at night
I know not to look
I'm afraid of the sight
As I crawl into bed
I hold my blankets tight
Just incase they try
Try to bite
Well you never know
They could, they might
I'm telling you the truth
My toys come alive at night.

Chantelle Warren (13)
Perryfields High School, Oldbury

Yellow

Yellow is the colour of brightness
Of the sunlight in the sky
Yellow is the ripe banana
A juicy lemon
Yellow is a happy memory
A sunflower's petals glistening in the sun
The colour of our lovable characters
Yellow is the colour of summer
The pot of colour at the end of the rainbow
The colour of money
The beauty of deserts
Of the pyramids in Giza
The boldness of a lion's mane
Yellow is a sandy beach
Yellow is simply happiness.

Amrita Phull (13)
Perryfields High School, Oldbury

View Of A 13-Year-Old

When I'm older. . .
I won't be traditional at my wedding
and wear white,
I'll be the opposite, and wear black,
the veil flooding behind me.
I'll walk up the isle in pink slippers,
and my bridesmaids will wear bikinis.
No one will sing bloody Jerusalem.
You will all chant Bohemian Rhapsody
and drink melted ice cubes.

When I'm older. . .
I won't hear the patter of tiny feet, I'll
adopt a baby orang-utan and
teach it to throw paper areoplanes at
the neighbours.

When I'm older. . .
My home will be circular, and the floor
will be a bouncy castle. My bathroom
won't have a roof so I can
take a shower when it rains.
And in the kitchen, I'll build a snowman
in the fridge.

When I'm older. . .
No one will wear black and my funeral,
everybody will be painted the colours of
the rainbow.
And in Heaven, I won't sit on a fluffy
cloud, I'll lie on the 'Easy Jet' aeroplane
and chat to God, and tell him how
I'll dare to be me when I'm older.

Emma Leppington (16)
Perryfields High School, Oldbury

A Blind Man

Being blind isn't easy,
Yes you have a guide dog,
But really, you don't know where you are.

Anybody could be staring at you,
Talking about you,
And you wouldn't suspect a thing.

Every day, going through life,
You don't know what today is going to hold,
You will have to wait and see.

Waking up, not seeing anything,
Not what you're wearing,
Not where you're going.

Time for breakfast,
Not seeing what you're about to eat,
You have to smell and taste it, rely on your senses.

What to do for the next couple of hours,
Any point in watching TV? I can't see it,
Again relying on my senses, this time my sense of hearing.

Time for tea, the same food scenario as breakfast,
I don't know what I'm about to eat,
Sad because I don't get a choice, whatever my bare hands find I eat.

Now I have to find my way upstairs, if I fall and die,
No one will care or look over me and protect me,
I will just have to hold my banister and pray to be safe.

Time for bed, I have to find my toothbrush and toothpaste,
Find my way to my bedroom, to my bed,
Without falling down the stairs.

What if somebody is there, silent, ready to kill me?
I don't know because I'm blind,
And there is no one there to watch over me.

Sunayna Shinh (12)
Queen Mary's High School, Walsall

A Day At The Beach

A day at the beach,
Is so much fun!
Laughter and excitement!
For everyone,
Breathe in the salty air,
Bit by bit,
On a donkey,
Is where you sit,
Playing games,
Licking lollies,
Little girls hugging their dollies!

Come on now,
That's enough excitement,
For the day,
Oh,
But we really want to stay,
If we don't go soon,
It will be dark!
Hurry up now,
And tomorrow I'll take you to the park!

Lauren Garbett (11)
Queen Mary's High School, Walsall

Friends

Friends are one,
Friends are two,
Friends like you are always true.
Friends are endless like a ring,
You can treasure it as one special thing.
What makes the perfect friend?
Someone who will stay till the end.
Someone who will stick next to you no matter what,
Or someone you have always got.
You can talk about secrets and dreams,
Or talk about the world as it seems.
To be a good friend you need to be true,
And always comfort a friend when they are blue.
To be a good friend you need to have trust,
And never let your relationship go a bust
To be a good friend you need to be you,
And always be there to see them through.
Friends are like butterflies,
They will always morph but their personalities will stay the same.
I have the perfect friend,
Her name is Mother.

Seliesha Chahal (12)
Queen Mary's High School, Walsall

My Eternity

I have never been surer of anything
Than the soaring entity
Surrounding me with your love.
The subtle power of
You iridescent hands, touching,
Stroking, silken touch.
It illuminates me, as innocence,
Which I can never be, though
In your eyes I am a God.
Portray your shining lust
Allow me to believe in myself again,
Regain my blind trust.
The light scorches my pallid flesh,
Your light a burning arrow
Piercing the black recesses of my heart.
You call me your dark lord,
I call you my blinding light.
Nothing I say can be so soft.
Light, golden touch.
Caress me with your warmth
And thaw the ice within.
Snakebite rhythm of my heart,
Dark and light flowing as one.
I enter, and you let me in.

Zoë Nicholson (17)
Queen Mary's High School, Walsall

Clouds

Clouds are fluffy,
Clouds are white.
Why do we never
See clouds at night?

Clouds are fat,
Clouds are thin.
Do you ever wonder
What lies within?

Clouds are tall,
Clouds are small.
Why are clouds
Any shape at all?

Clouds are bouncy,
Clouds are bold.
Do you wonder
What secrets they hold?

Clouds hold rain,
Clouds mask the sun.
What would happen
If they came undone?

Clouds in winter,
In summer too.
What do clouds
Conjure up for you?

Lauren Key (12)
Queen Mary's High School, Walsall

Dead To The World

I walk down the street, my life incomplete,
My heart torn to shreds, life was good,
But now it seems like everyone and everything has turned against me.

I walk along a path, up to a door and just stare at it
Until I find myself shaking with fear
I knock at his door, ready to apologise for something
That I can't remember the reason for.

The door stays closed, the house standing there in silence
The car's on the drive, the rubbish bins put out.
I walk away without a second thought. I feel the tears,
Gently making their way down my face.

I run to the park to hide my shameful face from the world. I turn my
Head to see children playing football. The ball is kicked my way,
As a small stubby boy makes his way over to collect the ball,
I say hello, but he doesn't respond.

Then I realize that I'm not really there. But where could I be?
It's too realistic to be a dream.
That's when I come to the conclusion. . .
I'm dead.

It must have happened whilst I was sleeping
Or did I die before my wedding day.
The wedding I thought I was at, wasn't a wedding
It was a funeral. . . Mine, no wonder he was crying.

Georgina Edkins (12)
Queen Mary's High School, Walsall

Diamond On A Savannah

A building tall on a desolate wasteland,
A sapling bud in a burned down wood,
A kite being flown on a high, high mountain;
A fish being born in a lake of mud.

A city grows on the barren country;
A forest returns to the charred remains;
The sky is awash with a thousand colours
And a stagnant lake thrives again.

On a summer night when the sun goes down
There shines but a single star.
Like a diamond dropped on a black savannah
Or a candle glowing from afar.

Kate Bradley (13)
Queen Mary's High School, Walsall

A Letter To Mommy

I'm sorry I was a bad girl.
I'm sorry I made your life hell.
I'm sorry I never made you happy.
They told me you weren't well.

It hurt me too, you know.
When you cried all day and night.
When you hit and smacked and scared me.
Why couldn't I make it right.

I'm sorry if you just didn't like me.
I'm sorry if I was never good enough.
I'm sorry that Daddy left you.
After he got you up the duff.

The doctors tell me you're getting better.
But you don't regret the things you did.
Even the day when the police were called.
And behind the sofa I hid.

This letter is for my mommy,
Who brought my into this life.
I just wanted to say, 'I hate you,'
For causing me that strife.

Stacy Knight (17)
Queen Mary's High School, Walsall

Behind Curtains

You're walking,
Walking towards me
You don't see me
You don't look

You would see me
If you tried
But you never do
I don't know you

I see the world through different eyes
Think about tomorrow
Think about today
But never the past

See the hurt
See the pain
See the hope
Forgotten of any gain

You don't care
You have a life
You don't see the curtains twitching
You don't want to peer inside

I want to help
If I could
But life is a play and I put on the act
Off you go, now
Curtains closed.

Daisy Hale (12)
Queen Mary's High School, Walsall

Heart To Heart

I could blow a kiss thousands of miles away,
And guarantee it would still reach you,
A rosy-pink velvet ribbon joining my heart to yours,
Our palms touch, our heart unite,
You will forever be my day,
And forever be my night,
The three words you whispered will stay in my heart,
(I love you) Nothing can tear us apart,
I shall shout from rooftops the name of my true love,
Hang your name by string around the neck of a dove,
No rings! No parties required!
You are the one and will always be the one I desire,
So, heart to heart.

Kanem Hutchinson (13)
Queen Mary's High School, Walsall

Our World

Everywhere around me, twenty-four hours a day,
Negative messages are being thrown my way.
Terrorism, extremists, war and racist views,
Famine, poverty and suffering on the news.

We all live in fear of a terrorist attack,
Suicide bombers with their weapons on their back,
Innocent civilians are dying - it's just not fair,
But these people aren't listening they don't even care.

All over the papers, blood and gore,
The innocent people dead from war.
They aren't asked if they want the war to start,
Yet it is their lives they ruin and tear apart.

Racial hate groups spreading their message on TV,
Trying to appeal to the likes of you and me,
Why can't people see, there is no superior race,
It really doesn't matter about the colour of your face.

I sit down in front of the telly, a tear comes to my eye,
I'm sitting here with chocolate, while starving children cry.
We try to help them out, raising money every day.
Why is there still people forced to live this way?

We sit in our lessons, we complain about a rule,
We don't appreciate how lucky we are, that we can go to school.
We moan about our homework, when it takes us the whole night,
None of us are grateful that we can all read and write.

These problems are ongoing, they'll never go away,
Unless some brave people stand up and have their say.
It's no use if you choose to sit there and wait,
We all need to pull together before it's too late.

Lauren Smith (13)
Queen Mary's High School, Walsall

My World

Walking down the stairs, I squeak
Going to the loo, I nod
Brushing my teeth, I shout
Walking the dog, I kick

As I walk down the street, people point and stare
People laugh and look, people mimic me.
I put up with it, if only they could see
How much their teasing upsets me.

In the dead of night, all on my own,
A little tear I shed.
I used to be outgoing,
But now my confidence is dead.

It's not my fault I yell,
Not my fault I swear
It is not my fault
That this condition is rare.

Not many people know,
The pain I feel inside,
And that most of the time
I want to run away and hide.

Why won't people try to ignore my Tourettes?
Treat me the same as everyone else?
Why won't people understand
That I am a human being?

Erin Charles (14)
Queen Mary's High School, Walsall

Too Much To Handle In A Day

I've just been involved in a hit and run,
I'm not quite sure what's just been done,
I see myself lying there,
Blood and dust in my hair,
I see the ambulance take me away,
As I chase, there's a few kids play,
When I reach me in my bed,
I've just realized I am dead,
I see my parents crying tears,
My sister and their other peers,
I wish I had looked before I crossed,
Because then, I could have bossed,
The children in my Year 6 class,
I would have taught them all about mass,
They will be really sad now,
Because now I will go and bow,
To they call the beloved one,
But first I shall go see my dad Jon,
I shall go see him in his gym,
For he loved me and I loved him.

Amy Kular (12)
Queen Mary's High School, Walsall

I Want You To Know. . .

I want you to know
Why I did what I did.
I was fifteen years old.
I was still a kid.

I never even knew him,
I never knew me.
One night of passion
Made life a misery.

Woke up the next morning,
Couldn't remember a thing.
I only found out you were coming,
A month after our fling.

I thought about us,
I thought about you.
What you could be like,
And what you could do.

I made my decision,
I've regretted it since then.
I dream about the clinic
I signed your life away with a pen.

I love you, my baby
I need you by my side.
I'm lying here on the beach,
I'll be with you by high tide.

I can't live without you.
I'm coming,
My darling.
Mom xxx

Chloë Guy (13)
Queen Mary's High School, Walsall

Friendship

Little stone won't get in the way,
Of running water flowing astray.
Mine and your friendship will
Always be here,
Although we're apart,
You'll be in my heart.

Bonnie Tsim (11)
Queen Mary's High School, Walsall

Sarah

The big black school gates,
These bring nothing but anger, pain and suffering to Sarah.

They are a big reminder of the school bully,
The bully makes Sarah tremble with fear,
Her voice, her look makes Sarah cry.
Sarah's eyes have more than a tear
As the bully corners Sarah and turns her face as flat as a pie.

Sarah's friends do not believe her,
They say the bully is too kind
But Sarah knows in one foul swoop. . .
These thoughts being chaos to her mind.
. . . Sarah dropped down into a stoop.

The bully's fist went back for the punch
When all of a sudden there was a cry.
Sarah looked up to see the big bully take,
A look at a girl hung up by her tie.
Sarah thought this was her lucky break.

Sarah ran and shouted, 'Bye loser!'
The bully saw her and grabbed her back,
She pushed Sarah against the wall,
Pulled a knife out of her rucksack
She said, 'Take it back or you will fall.'

'No,' shouted Sarah as loud as she could
She'd stood up for herself like she said she would
The bully pulled back the knife,
And with one loud thud,
The bully had taken Sarah's life.

Blood poured onto the floor
As Sarah's hurtful life was no more.

Caitlin Clarke (13)
Queen Mary's High School, Walsall

Her And Her Fiancé

As you sit there in your heartache,
All you can do is weep.
For when you put the bullet to his head,
The blood began to seep.

It wouldn't stop for a long, long time,
And when it did, there was no more,
And as you see your fiancé dead,
You drop fainting to the floor.

You realise what you have done,
And lifting the bottle to your head,
You drink all of the poison,
And instantly you are dead.

Laura Pincher (12)
Queen Mary's High School, Walsall

Friends

Near or far,
You will always be together,
The secrets you share,
Forever and ever,

Special bonds of happiness,
Memories so clear,
Laughter and joyfulness,
Bravery and fear,

Looking out for one another,
Every single day,
Years will fly by,
It will never go away,

Even at the very end,
They will still be close at heart,
Always and a day,
You will never be apart.

Alysia Dyke (11)
Queen Mary's High School, Walsall

The Silent Assassin

The lights are dark,
there's no escape
from the crowds below.
I pull the bow
across the strings
to make the heavenly sounds.
To them, this is real
but everything to me,
this reality is fake.
The lives that rule me,
show no fear or peace.
I may not have a voice
and be as quiet as a mouse,
but still, I make my thoughts clear,
my cello is a weapon,
it hypnotises them all.
I take them away
all the lifeless bodies,
and make my judgments right.
The sword that hangs on the wall
is comfortably gripped in my hands.
The blade that digs
into flesh and blood
has everything to do with me.
The redness shines,
from the moon,
and into the darkness of my heart.
I tried to release them
from their sins and all,
but there's no escape. . .

Vincy Lee (12)
Queen Mary's High School, Walsall

The Man From Blackheath

There was a man from Blackheath
No one liked him because of his black teeth.
Wherever he walked
People would talk
About his rather unappealing walk.
He was as tall as a giraffe
And still owned a café
As much as he bent down,
He could never get through the door, so he frowned
He looked like an old man
Because of his unusual tan.
He covered it with mustard
And shouted, 'It's better than custard.'
He lived in the United States
So he decided to call his son Ben Bates.
It was obvious that Kieth
Needed to clean his teeth!

Anika Loi (12)
Queen Mary's High School, Walsall

Red

Love is red,
But so is anger.
Love fulfils your heart,
Anger bubbles up in one's eyes.
Red is the colour of my love for the world,
Red is the colour of my sadness and
Sorrow for the neglected and poor.
Red is fire and roses.

Taranpreet Kaur Sohal (11)
Queen Mary's High School, Walsall

A Chance

When you have a chance,
Then you let it slip away,
When you totally regret it,
Hoping that chance will return someday.

Then you stay up all night,
Thinking about how stupid you've been,
Then you wonder what might've happened,
It would've been a talent everyone would've seen.

If you didn't sieze that chance,
Then no one would know what you can show,
It makes you think sometimes,
Would you brightly shine or let it blow?

But when that chance is given once again,
Will you take someone else's advice
Or will you think deeply
And consider it twice?

Nikita Joshi (11)
Queen Mary's High School, Walsall

The Lesson

The teacher walked in
And he tripped over a bin.

The teacher said, 'Do your work or die,
While I eat a pie,
Are you ready to say bye
And wear your tie.'

He hit a boy,
With his toy,
He killed his class,
With some mass,
Now let that be a lesson to you.

Anil Bansal (11)
Smestow School, Castlecroft

My Similes

An acorn as smooth as a puppy's ear.
A leaf as rough as sandpaper.
A fir tree as spiky as a porcupine.
A red leaf as bright as fire.
A conker as shiny as a brown leather boot.
A leaf just like the shape of a heart.
A piece of holly as sharp as a tiger's tooth.
A leaf as soft as a piece of felt.
A fir cone that looks like a hedgehog.

Katy Skobel (11)
Smestow School, Castlecroft

The Lesson

The PE lesson had started,
Miss Slack walked into the hall.
'Today's lesson is gymnastics,
Now do a handstand against the wall!'

The children were surprised,
By Miss Slack's shrill cries,
So they did the handstands anyway.
But Jill couldn't do it,
She cried, 'I blew it,'
However Miss Slack gave her detention come what may.

Thomas was hungry,
So he went to his backpack
Evil Miss Slack saw him,
And gave him a smack.

Daniel walked over,
'I'm going to Dover,
I'll dismiss myself Miss, don't worry.'
'Oh no you don't,
You can't do it, you won't,'
Miss Slack ran after him in a flurry.

'Don't worry Miss,
Soon I'll be back.'
Miss Slack pulled out a belt,
It went whirl and whack.

The bell suddenly rang,
With a great loud clang
Miss Slack gave an evil growl.
'Class is dismissed'
Miss Slack hissed,
'Remember I'm on the prowl.'

Ophiah Deans (11)
Smestow School, Castlecroft

Autumn

Autumn leaves on the ground,
Red and brown all around.
Most of them are as glossy as silk,
And feathers, as soft as a quilt!

Branches as thick as bones,
But not as pretty as fir cones.
An acorn like a polished shoe,
The colours disgusting but that'll do.

The outside of acorn cups is like speed bumps,
They're everywhere! They look like lumps.
Conkers start off green then shread their shell,
From the tree it has fell.

People wrap up in hats and scarves,
And huddle round fires in hearths.
As autumn draws to an end,
And winter's coming, it's just round the bend.

Tarnia Osborne (11)
Smestow School, Castlecroft

The Autumn Poem

The dandelion leaf grows,
Grows as the wind flows,
The daisy grows,
Grows at the speed of grass,
The leaves flow off trees,
Just as the trees flee from the ground.

The leaves fall,
On trees so tall,
The leaves fall with all their might,
When they're down they're alright.

The wind blows the leaves,
Leaves that are crispy as crisps,
As the leaves are gone,
The sad faces are there
There in the disappointment

There's a leaf, and another leaf
The sad faces are now smiles.

Ryan Silwood (11)
Smestow School, Castlecroft

Autumn Poem

Here comes autumn leaves as red as fire,
Watch them as they roll down, like a tyre.
Here comes the rain trickling from the sky,
Teardrops from God as if someone told a lie.

Here comes acorns falling from a tree,
When they are falling, they are falling on me.
Here comes hazelnuts green and ripe,
People describing its prickly type.

Here comes winter with the frost,
It covers flowers, which are now lost.
Here comes spring, with energy and powers,
Something is growing, it's more flowers.

Here comes summer, nearly autumn again,
It's going round and round like a choo-choo train.
When, oh when will this ever stop?
Here comes harvest, gathering more crops.

Gurgeena Bhadal (11)
Smestow School, Castlecroft

Forbidden Beauty

Walking alone in the rain,
Isolation surrounding my body.

Only the words of one can keep me sane,
The beauty of voice,
The beauty of words,
Alone but surrounded by the beauty of someone I'll never know.

Being an outsider in a world full of beauty,
I'll guess my mind will never be spilt,
And my true feelings for others will never be known.

'How do you influence me?'
A question that eternally echoes in my mind.

Even if the answer's never known,
In my heart I know your words,
Your words,
Are the ones that kept me sane.

Michael Williams (15)
Smestow School, Castlecroft

Autumn Poem

Autumn multicoloured leaves
Brown, green that fall from the trees

Leaves crunching under my foot
Acorns, conkers let's have a look

Pinecones on the floor
Leaves blowing up your door

Lots of colours in the air
Red and yellow orange fair

The little squirrel with acorns galore
Hidden away in his winter store

October brings the end of BST
Winter woollens for you for you and me.

Hollie Brown (11)
Smestow School, Castlecroft

The Leaf Poem

A brown crisp leaf as dry as an
old house which has been up
for thousands of years.
The garden is an old
ruin with millions of
leaves falling off the trees.

Michael Jukes
Smestow School, Castlecroft

My Autumn Poem

Leaves started to fall
As the trees stood tall
Autumn on its way
Hip, hip, Hooray

Girls are exited
As they get to wear their new boots
All the animals come out of their homes
As the squirrels start to scoot!

Mothers have started cooked
The lovely Christmas pudding
It is getting colder
Also getting darker

Christmas is finally here
Children are opening their presents
What a surprise they get
As one of them gets a Christmas pet.

Abbie Jane Robinson (11)
Smestow School, Castlecroft

The Lesson

The teacher walked in
And tripped over the bin
The teacher hit a boy
But the boy hit him with a toy
And the teacher said, 'Go to the headteacher Roy
you very little boy!'

The teacher took a gun
The bullet bounced off and hit the teacher's thumb
The teacher died
But no one cried
Everyone lived happily ever after
With lots and lots of laughter.

Vishaal Leekha (11)
Smestow School, Castlecroft

Textured Colours

A
red leaf
as crispy as
a crisp being
eaten. The leaf burning
bright as a hot fire when
they pull off the trees
on to the very green
grass.

Joe Ellam (11)
Smestow School, Castlecroft

A Time Like A Place

A time like a place between black and white
Where day is not day and night is not night
Where coldness burns and where fire freezes
Where you can be whole while torn to pieces
Entwined yet opposed are lovers and foes
With hope we go on that joys outweigh woes

Fleeting is the fun in the youth of life
For time turns bliss to misery and strife
Wrath consumes the soul impetuously
Wanting to slay and slaughter vehemently
Where once lips did procure kisses tender
Words malicious in form you now render

Yet darkness of mind never seemed so fine
Would you have sugar in your blood and wine?

Sophie Deery (16)
Solihull Sixth Form College, Solihull

Racism

Racism is one person
Making fun of another
Because of their colour.

Police are more likely
To arrest a black person
Than a white person.

It is unfair that black people
Are seen as troublemakers.
When they are British citizens
Just as much as white people.

Andrew Osborne (12)
The Orchard Centre PRU, Wolverhampton

Footballing Racism

At football games there are a lot of racists,
There is a huge list,
But racism is not good,
You know you should not do it bud!

You should not judge by the colour,
Because the cells are getting fuller.

It does not matter if you're white,
You can't even tell in the night,
And it doesn't matter if you're not the same,
We are all here to watch the game.

You should not judge by the colour,
Because the cells are getting fuller.

You go to the games to watch football,
And when we all get along it will be cool,
You should judge on personality,
Come on and see the reality.

You should not judge by the colour,
Because the cells are getting fuller.

I hope you have listened to what I have said,
I hope it goes to your head.

Daniel Howells (13)
The Orchard Centre PRU, Wolverhampton

Child Abuse

Why do people do such things?
Why is it done today?
Why are child abusers amongst us?
Why won't they go away?

Children want to tell people,
But they are just too scared,
They are always crying,
And think what it would be like if someone cared.

Why are abusers such vulgar people?
Why are they so sad?
Why do they use the Internet?
Why do they make it so bad?

If someone should approach you,
With ideas that are wrong,
You should go and tell someone,
This will make you strong!

Why are people so evil?
Why do they prey on a child?
Why; they are adults?
Why are they so wild?

Such people should be locked up,
And the key thrown well away,
They should be imprisoned,
Away from the light of day!

Joshua Williams (13)
The Orchard Centre PRU, Wolverhampton

Fears

What are fears?
Are they always bad?
They can make you happy,
They can make you sad.

It's fun to be scared,
When on a fair ride,
The adrenalin rush,
Makes you feel good inside.

But if you are scared,
Of everyday things,
It makes you unhappy,
It makes your head ring.

You can be frightened of spiders,
The dark or the light,
Dark, dirty water,
Or even of night.

You can be scared of going out,
Or even staying in,
You can be frightened of people in the street,
Or fingers or even feet.

But I'm doing this poem in my seat,
Some kids are scared of being beat,
Fears can be overcome,
If you've got any problems tell someone.

Ryan Weston (13)
The Orchard Centre PRU, Wolverhampton

Teenage Pregnancy

Why do teenage girls get pregnant?
Why do they have sex so young?
Why do they want a baby?
Don't they know how hard it is?

It happened to me.
I went through it.
I was scared
From the beginning to the end.
I gave my baby away.
I was upset about giving my baby away.

I am now happy but I am thinking about the baby all the time.

Elizabeth Homer (13)
The Orchard Centre PRU, Wolverhampton

Disability

I see the people stare at me
Everywhere I go
It's not my fault the way I am
But people judge me though.

I am in a wheelchair
I am deaf and I cannot see.
If all the people in this world
Were only to hear it from me.

Being disabled is very hard
Looking after myself and my life.
People walk down the road
Not seeing my strife.

Now all I am asking
Is for you to see.
Do not judge me anymore
Please just respect me!

The moral of my poem
Is just to say
Please respect disabled people
Respect them in every way.

Samantha Hughes (13)
The Orchard Centre PRU, Wolverhampton

Homelessness

Never knowing where you'll be
Today, tomorrow or next week
Your future is bleak
Sunday
Scare me
Monday
Makes me cry
Tuesday
Selling 'Big Issue'
Wednesday
Why me?
Thursday
Tired out
Friday
It's not forever
Saturday
Robbing food
Sunday, here we go again.

Christopher Parker (12)
The Orchard Centre PRU, Wolverhampton

England

Sometimes bombings
Sometimes stabbings
Sometimes crashes
Sometimes riots
Sometimes fires
Sometimes deaths.

Usually crowding
Usually travel problems
Usually bad neighbours
Usually graffiti on walls
Usually dogs barking
Usually crowding in streets when football matches.

Not many animals escaping from zoos
Not many police chases
Not many breakdowns
Not many earthquakes
Not many twisters.

Mikey Howells (11)
The Orchard Centre PRU, Wolverhampton

Talk Of My Presence

Talk of my presence.
Tell me I'm here.
Hold me close,
Fight away my fears.

We are the definition,
Of death.
We are the reason,
Perfection was not kept.

Further away is past,
My future; wanting to hold
I realise at last,
My future was sold.

Feeling that shiver,
I once felt.
Hearing the ice,
In my heart . . . melt.

Is this not love,
If it cannot be located?
Is it not love,
If it cannot be stated?

Talk of my presence,
Tell be I'm here.
Notice my voice,
Uncover my tears.

Elizabeth Price (15)
The Orchard Centre PRU, Wolverhampton

School Dinners?

Die horrid food,
It makes my friend dead,
You can feed Africa with it,
D is for disgusting,
And F for failure,

The food kills you if you eat it,
And don't you dare to eat it,
But there is one thing to say,
Jamie Oliver,
Stop already.

Jordan Dearn (13)
The Orchard Centre PRU, Wolverhampton

True Friends

Friendship is a special thing, full of
laughter, fun and tears,
your secrets, your wishes and all your fears
which will show over the years.
Overtime friends will come and go,
and all our feelings will start to show.

Our friendship will always stay strong
and true,
because I am unique and so are you.
There's nothing nicer than someone who
shares,
by showing their feelings for how
much they care.

A friend is someone who stands by you
through the good times and the bad,
and lets you share all your true feelings
when you're down and sad.
Friends are just like angels sent from above,
and come down and give us all their love.

Stacey Kendrick (13)
Warley High School College of Sport, Oldbury

Tsunami

No one knew it was coming,
No one expected it,
But a few seconds later,
A monstrous twenty foot wave,
Destroyed everything that came its way, with a
Loud roaring voice.
It came so fast with swirling anger,
There was no time to think of how to escape.
It swept away many lives,
It swept away many smiles,
It swept away all the happiness,
And left behind the sorrowness,
After nature's attack, no one could do anything.
As the angry ocean calmed down,
The only thing you could hear were crying sounds.
Children who survived were crying for their parents,
Adults who survived were praying to God, hoping their children will be alive. . .
 . . . But all their hopes and tears come to waste.

As time passed by,
Everyone was fine,
All the pain and sorrow,
Were dreadful memories.
People might think we have fallen down,
But they are wrong.
But we will rise again,
Higher than before.

Priya Thamilarasan (13)
Warley High School College of Sport, Oldbury

It's A Secret

Bang goes the door, he's back
I lie in the black
In my bed
Sometimes wishing I was dead
I close my eyes I don't even peep
And cry myself to sleep
But no sooner as he came he's gone again
Leaving me in loads of pain
Not allowed to tell
If anyone asks I fell
The tears run down my face
That's the only trace
No one else can see
The way he hurts me
Maybe one day the pain will end
But I'll never be his friend.

Demi Woodward (13)
Warley High School College of Sport, Oldbury

This World

Racist comments, calling names
Stupid wars, crashing planes
People arguing, fighting too
But there is nothing I can do
People getting drunk, taking drugs
Dropping food, being litter bugs
People doing bad and committing crimes
Hardly anything is done, maybe nothing sometimes
This is what our world is all about
Many more things happen no doubt
If I went on I would be here all day
So I'm going to zip my mouth up and nothing else I will say.

Rachel Bayliss (13)
Warley High School College of Sport, Oldbury

The Bank Robber (Me)

I can't believe I'm doing this,
Why didn't I think?
This man is innocent,
And could be dead in a wink.

I am a nice guy I swear I am,
Believe me and understand.
I need the money really bad,
So I have a gun resting in my hand.

Finger on the trigger, ready to roll,
Watching the man crack the safe bar.
Grabbed all of the lovely money,
But in need of a getaway car.

Grabbed him by the neck took him outside,
Loaded the gun, it let out a click.
The police lowered their guns,
Get out the car and let me in quick.

I drove off at full speed,
Wind blowing my hair.
I pushed out the hostage,
Not even a care!

The coppers followed,
Flashing sirens and alarms at me.
I knew I had no chance,
So I plunged into the sea!

That was the end of me.

Ayshea Ravenscroft (13)
Warley High School College of Sport, Oldbury

Dad

The hurt and the pain
I hope it never happens again
The way I'm feeling inside
I just wanted to hide
He said he wouldn't leave
But when he did I couldn't breathe
He lied, he lied
I died, I died inside
The screams and the shouts
And then he walked out
Out in the rain
I never saw him again
No more memories of happiness and fun
All because of what he had done!

Ashlee Carver (13)
Warley High School College of Sport, Oldbury

My Prayer To God

Hi God it's me again,
I'm wondering if you see,
The pain and all the hurt,
My mum and dad bring to me.

I don't know why they hit me,
When I haven't done anything wrong,
What they do to me is torture,
And it taunts me all day long.

People around me see it,
But they just let it slide,
Because nobody really notices,
How much it hurts inside.

People see this everyday.
But choose to ignore it instead,
And that's why thousands of kids like me,
Are beaten till they're dead.

Gemma Brookes (13)
Warley High School College of Sport, Oldbury

Through The Eyes Of A Mouse

Gosh those people are big,
Ahhh! What's that a twig?
Looking for food is an obstacle course,
My life is worse than a horse.
I flit from door to door,
Wanting more and more.
Then I get chased out of the room,
With this great big thing, a broom.
Trying to get through this little hole,
Thank goodness I'm not a mole.
There's plenty of cheese I suppose,
I could eat that if I chose.
But I want something tasteful,
My I'm ungrateful.
There's not a big choice of food here,
Excuse me I need to scratch my ear,
Ahhh that's better, but my stomach's still grumbling,
Next I'll hear it rumbling.
Then there's that great big cat,
I'd just love to whack off his head with a bat.
He's got whiskers longer than me,
And something flies off him, a flea.
Then he tries to grab my tail,
Sometimes I just drop and wail.
At least I'm not a fat little mouse,
The cat makes sure of that in this house.
Anyway I'll have to go back to my cheese and my treasure,
At least that will be to my pleasure!

Yours truly,
Pompom.

Ivinder Virdee (13)
Warley High School College of Sport, Oldbury

My Story

Here I am in the corner of the room,
Sitting here staring into gloom,
Tears rolling down my face,
Knowing that I am a disgrace,
I hear footsteps coming closer to me,
Scared to death, I always be,
Door opens,
He walks over... closer and
Closer I will never be free,
I know in my head,
These words in my mind . . .
Beat me till I'm black and blue,
But I know that inside I am
Stronger than you!
Will always be there until . . .
I die.

Danielle Watton (13)
Warley High School College of Sport, Oldbury

Far Away But Here In My Heart!

He made me laugh all the time,
He took me places, learned me to read and rhyme,
He loved me so much, and I loved him too,
I loved to play my favourite game when I was little, peek-a-boo!
Why did he have to go away, why oh why?
Although he will be happy and the angels will teach him to fly.
I miss him dearly.
My eyes have watered, I can't see clearly.
Nanny misses you too and so does everyone,
Why did you have to go? It felt like my life had just begun.
I know Heaven is far from here and we're very far apart.
But my grandad, your love will always be in my heart.
As time may pass,
But our love for you will always last,
And I know you are watching us to see how we are.
As I still remember those day trips out in your car.
Now I wipe my tears upon my face,
I think about Grandad in that heavenly place.
And Grandad I just want you to know we all love you!
And we always will do!

Lydiarose Smith (13)
Warley High School College of Sport, Oldbury

Autumn

When leaves start to fall
When conkers are collected
Autumn is our kind of season,

Red, brown, gold and yellow
Are the colours which blend together

Animals feed then search and try to
Find a home to fall in a big sleep
Because sleep is. . .
Right round the corner.

Charlotte Woolls (13)
Warley High School College of Sport, Oldbury

Far From Home

I woke up. Where am I?
all I remember is being shouted at and shoved into this place,
I am so small but why did I get hurt?
All I ever did was be funny, playful and loving,
I loved my friend, he was tall and fun to play with,
but when this all started I wondered, does he not love me?
he'd shout and hit me then I'd wake up,
with no recollection of what happened.
I scratched the top of this small and dark space.
I looked out and cried out,
some people came over there was three all hooded,
they kicked, I fell out,
they shook me about,
why did they want me out!
Finally they left, I feel so bad,
what have I done to all these people hitting me, hurting me?
I'm here alone in the dark,
where am I? I don't know, it feels so far from home,
I've got my fur to keep me warm.
I'll just start walking, maybe I'll get back soon.

AZB (13)
Warley High School College of Sport, Oldbury

My Sticky End

To my not so special friend.
This is about my tragic end.
My story began not long ago
When everything made sense and I went with the flow.
I lived in a small stable.
I was fit and able.
But not good enough for you.
I was sold to an evil man.
He stuck me in a cold old van.
I was took far and wide.
I was dropped off at a slaughter
Axes and knifes flew at my neck
I was a total wreck
My bones were crushed to make glue
That's all thanks to you
So this is the end of my story,
So when you do use that glue I'll be thinking of you.

Emma Bate (13)
Warley High School College of Sport, Oldbury

My Life With Autism And Down's Syndrome

From the day I was born I was special,
All of my family kept telling me so,
I always knew I was different,
But it wasn't until school I knew how.

All my classmates were talking but not me,
They ignored my noise when I tried,
The had no understanding of what I tried to say,
I was sad when they all wouldn't play.

In my world my family all love me,
At school my class think I'm strange,
They don't like me rocking when I get upset,
It's then when they call me bad names.

My teacher thinks Down's syndrome children,
Like to be cuddled and fussed,
But I have autism as well as this,
It hurts me when people touch me.

In class I am always told, 'Look at me!'
But it hurts my eyes doing that,
I want to be in my own little world,
With no one bothering me.

Now I'm 13 I have learned to behave as my teachers expect me to,
But at home in room I can rock and flap and no one ever complains,
I will never learn as quickly as others,
But I'm happy just being me.

Society thinks 'Special' people,
Should always be hidden away,
Thank goodness my family loves me,
And treat me like an equal every day.

Emma Harley (13)
Warley High School College of Sport, Oldbury

Friends Forever Even Though We Are Far Apart

All our late nights,
Our big sleepover,
Going to town spending all our money,
All of this I will remember because of our time together.

All our crazy pictures,
Our silly laughs,
Not one little argument,
Because we are so close as friends but so far by land.

Because we are so far apart,
What would we do without MSN?
Talking about boys, clothes and hair,
Helping each other through the bad days.

We are friends that live so far apart,
We see each other in the holidays, nothing more, nothing less,
Why does it have to be like this, why can't you just live by me?
Friends forever even though we are so far apart.

Charlie Morrall (13)
Warley High School College of Sport, Oldbury

Homeless

Here I am lying on the dirty, damp street,
Cold and bare, nothing on my feet.

Nowhere to go, no one to see,
Could someone please feel sorry for me?

Here I am all alone,
With no place to call my very own.

I'm hungry, I'm starving, I need something to eat,
Could someone please put some money down by my feet?

Clothing and blankets would make a good start,
But I need food in my belly and love in my heart.

No one to kiss or say it's alright,
No one to be there all through the night.

I wonder why I've been put on this Earth,
Is it to sit in my own filth and dirt?

I hope someday someone will come for me,
So I can be loved and out of poverty.

Mollie Bastable (13)
Warley High School College of Sport, Oldbury

Friendship

I hope that you and I will never be apart
If so, in distance, I hope not in heart.

I'm glad I have friend like you
Can trust and tell anything to
Likes me for who I am
Never lets me down
You deserve a best friend's crown.

A person I can look up to
I'll always be here for you
I'd like to mean as much to you
As you mean to me.

I hope that you and I will never be apart
If so, in distance, I hope not in heart.

Lucy Botfield (14)
Whiteheath Education Centre, Rowley Regis

The Dentist's

Ring! ring! goes the telephone,
I don't like it here, I want to go home!

There I am sitting in the chair,
What is he doing? This isn't fair!

In he goes talks some gobbledygook!
In my mouth goes some horrible gloop!

Ouch! What's that? You said it wouldn't hurt!
'You little coward!' said my brother Kurt.

There! All finished. It's time to leave,
A sigh of relief I did heave!

Forms were filled in, nearly there,
What were they for? I didn't care!

I made my escape, I got in the car,
Home is round the corner, it's not very far.

Elizabeth Worton (13)
Whiteheath Education Centre, Rowley Regis

Gary The Dog

Gary is a little dog,
He's always sleeping like a log,
At the window he always barks,
Round his food dish he always larks.

Gary is a little mutt,
His whole body is the colour of soot,
Call his name and he will run,
As fast as the bullet out of a gun.

Gary is a little friend,
Eating and sleeping until the end,
He is a strong little mutt and he sure can bite,
He will never lose a fight.

So all in all Gary is a cool dog,
He almost caught and killed a frog,
But regardless of how bitey he can be,
He will forever and always belong to me.

Kyle Roberts (13)
Whiteheath Education Centre, Rowley Regis

A Japanese Boy

Chang Li is a Japanese boy
with a brand new Japanese toy
its name is Robo-Raptor
and it's going to need to be looked after.

However the boy
did not like this Japanese toy
because it needed to be looked after
so he chucked it in the wardrobe till after.

After soon came
the boy was playing on a video game
however he still did not want to play with it
so he told his mom he would be back in a bit.

He took it to a flat car park
however by now it was dark
he knew homeless people lived here
and then he gave it to them and disappeared.

He did a good thing giving to the poor and
guess who was watching, it was Santa Claus.

Lee Dyson (13)
Whiteheath Education Centre, Rowley Regis

Winter

December brings the winter chills.
With extra jumpers and heating bills.
Christmas time will be here soon
With festive cheer to brighten the gloom.

January is the month that shines
With glittering snow, but that's just fine,
And snowmen sitting on the ground
In their top hats, don't make a sound.

Next is February, frosty days,
Now the snow is going away
But rainy days have still to come
To spread their wetness and hide the sun.

Amy Dyson (13)
Whiteheath Education Centre, Rowley Regis

Young Writers Information

We hope you have enjoyed reading this book - and that you will continue to enjoy it in the coming years.

If you like reading and writing poetry drop us a line, or give us a call, and we'll send you a free information pack.

Alternatively if you would like to order further copies of this book or any of our other titles, then please give us a call or log onto our website at
www.youngwriters.co.uk

Young Writers Information
Remus House
Coltsfoot Drive
Peterborough
PE2 9JX

(01733) 890066